VALIDATE ME!

How my mom's hoarding kind of messed me up.

VALIDATE ME!

How my mom's hoarding kind of messed me up.

Melissa K.M. Patton

Published by Melissa K.M. Patton
2014

Copyright © 2014 by Melissa K.M. Patton

All rights reserved. This book or any portion thereof may not be reproduced or used in any manner whatsoever without the express written permission of the publisher except for the use of brief quotations in a book review or scholarly journal.

First Printing: 2014

Published by Melissa K.M. Patton
Manufactured in the United States of America

ISBN 978-1-304-95774-0

https://www.facebook.com/ValidateMeBook

Screaming Flea Productions, A&E, and "Hoarders" are trademarked names and have been mentioned with express written permission from the producers and the network.

Cover and author photography by Debra Heschl Photography.

For my daughters,
with love.

And for fellow
daughters and sons of hoarders,
with hope.

Contents

Introduction 1
Chapter 1: Memories 3
Chapter 2: Hoarders 19
Chapter 3: Hoarding Hurts 31
Chapter 4: Sessions 41
Chapter 5: Science 65
Chapter 6: Boys 73
Chapter 7: Normal 85
Conclusion 103
Bibliography 105
Acknowledgments 107

Introduction

"Do I have to respond to every little thing you say? Sometimes I don't have a response, but I heard what you said!"

The curt words from my high school best friend stung and embarrassed me. I had been talking about something inconsequential – don't even remember the context now – and she said nothing in response. So I asked her if she was "mad at me or something." Given the exasperated tone of her response (that I still remember like it happened yesterday), my tone was likely just as unpleasant.

In high school, I was *constantly* worried that people were mad at me. Friends. Classmates. Teachers. Strangers. Everyone. I went around claiming I didn't care what people thought of me, but that could not have been further from the truth. I did not realize it back then, but time and experience have made it evident to me that everything I did was in pursuit of acceptance and approval.

To everyone I have ever known, I'm sorry.

VALIDATE ME!

Chapter 1: Memories

When I was born, the library/office in my parents' house was converted into my nursery. By converted, I mean my mom and dad put a crib, dresser, and rocking chair into the room, but never got rid of the large metal desk or tall metal bookcases that lined the walls. But it was sufficient for a baby, and at least I had Care Bear curtains.

As a small child, when I was at home I played in a small space on the living room floor. It was cramped, but I just figured I had a lot of toys. My dad would sit in his straw rocking chair and watch TV. I don't remember if we ever had a couch (an old picture of me as a toddler suggests that we did), but I do remember being able to comfortably watch TV in the living room together as a family. We ate some meals together in the eat-in kitchen – me in my high chair, and my parents at the little green-top table. My mom was a phenomenal cook and baked the most amazing banana muffins. She made Mickey Mouse banana pancakes for me on weekends and carved out a happy face in every new tub of margarine. Sometimes she picked fresh, ripe papayas from our tree, and served them, too.

We had two Siamese cats; one was friendly, one was not. Mom liked to sew and often made us matching dresses. Each Christmas, we would get a real Christmas tree. Mom would decorate it, and there would be presents under it on Christmas morning.

As I got older, Mom started working late a lot, and I was getting more involved in Girl Scouts and gymnastics. On my free nights you could find me outside riding my bike or rollerblading with the neighborhood kids. Dad and I started bonding over regular trips to the library, park, golf, the Sanrio section of what used to be Holiday Mart, and fast food. Around this time we started eating out more, or my dad and I would eat frozen meals on my parents' bed, where we started watching most of our TV. The living room and kitchen were gradually becoming increasingly cluttered by empty boxes, plastic and Styrofoam cups, containers, jars, and egg cartons that my mom was hanging on to for "proofs of purchase" and various future projects. We spent less and less time in those common areas until eventually we had no choice but to avoid them all together. The living room TV was the one with cable, though, so when I wanted to watch movies or music videos, I would have to clear the space in front of the TV and find a place to sit. I think at one point there was a stool…or I would just sit on a sturdy box.

Tangent: Speaking of memories with my dad, I wrote the following blog post in honor of my dad for Father's Day 2012.

Spotlight on… Dad (June 2012)
In honor of Father's Day coming up on June 17th, I wanted to share some fond memories I have had with my dad over the years. My parents are still together, but my mom worked a lot when I was growing up, so most of my childhood was spent with my dad. I have always been, and always will be, a daddy's girl.

These are somewhat in chronological order.

- Teaching me how to ride a bicycle
- Singing Peter, Paul, & Mary in the car together on many drives to elementary school
- Daddy-Daughter camping when I was a Brownie Girl Scout
- Taking me to the park to push me on the swing, fly a kite, play basketball
- Setting out my bath towel and toothbrush for me every night
- Accompanying me as I walked around my entire town selling Girl Scout cookies
- Hanging out at his office, visiting the warehouse guys
- Dog sitting at his sister's house after school…with junk food and TV
- Pizza Hut and Taco Bell after school
- Dave's Ice Cream after gymnastics
- Teaching me how to play chess
- Teaching me how to play golf, and taking me to the driving range
- Teaching me to drive and then taking me to get my driver's license
- Watching my high school basketball games
- Hearing that he started going to church
- Walking me down the aisle when I got married
- Holding his first grandchild

I have countless other memories with him that may not be as "fond," but still conjure deep appreciation, nonetheless: spending hours at the library with me, helping me write my first research papers in elementary school; four years of gymnastics practice and meets; weekly trips to the Orthodontist; installing my ceiling fan; chauffeuring me all over the island until I could drive (mall, friends' houses, State Fair, movies, birthday parties, etc.); getting lost on Maui...

I firmly believe that you cannot FULLY comprehend the sacrificial love of a (good) parent until you walk in their shoes. Sure, as you get older – and especially as you become responsible for your own finances – you realize more and more how much they've done for you; but to see how much they gave up for you, so you could have a decent childhood and allow you to do all the things YOU wanted to do...I think that's hard to truly know until you've started making those sacrifices for your own child(ren). I am starting to understand this more each day. When I review just this short list, it is very clear to me that he limited his free time to allow me to pursue my own interests and make sure I wasn't constantly with a babysitter. He could have easily said, "Screw this, your mom's not here to take care of you, why should the burden fall on me?" but he never did. Not once. He was (is!) a good father. He still had his interests, but he found a way to balance it with taking care of me – and I know I was a handful at times!

To my dad... Thank you!

I just wanted to include that as a demonstration of how most of my good memories happened outside of our home. Keep reading and you will understand why.

By the time I was about thirteen years old, the sewing room, which had always been full of stuff, became impenetrably blocked off by boxes of who-knows-what, and little paths throughout the rest of the house were formed where there was once floor. Mom stopped cooking. Getting a Christmas tree became a battle that involved weeks of moving the clutter around so we would have just enough space for it atop the card table that sat amongst a pile of stuff in the middle of the living room. (Most of that stuff ended up in bags and boxes in the carport, which ultimately stopped housing the car.) The tree would go on the table, and Mom would decorate it with an eclectic variety of ornaments that followed no theme but had significant sentimental value, such as ones I had made in school. We were lucky if we got our tree set up a full week before Christmas. Eventually even that became impossible. One Christmas, we threw the presents in the car and drove to my dad's office, where I sat on the floor near a fake tree and we opened our gifts there.

Path through living room towards the kitchen

No one ever came to our house to visit or stay over. Anyone who did happen to catch a glimpse of the inside of our house always seemed shocked at how "messy" it was or how much stuff we had.

Living room

I desperately loved going to my friends' houses. Even if their houses were no bigger than mine, it always felt like a mansion to me because they had so much space. With wide eyes, I would always say, "Wow, you have such a nice house." They had walls. And carpet. Their clothes were in their closets. Their doors closed. Ours couldn't close because they were jammed open with boxes or things hanging from them and in the doorway. I had a screen door on my bedroom that my parents had no way of replacing with a normal door even if they wanted to. (I wanted to. Imagine the awkwardness of my teen years.) Besides, I had "a nice breeze" that my parents did not want to cut off.

My sense of reality was warped. I did not understand it, I just knew my house was messy. *I hated my house.*

Kitchen sink beyond the piles

By the time I was in high school, you could barely walk through the living room and kitchen without knocking down some precariously-balanced tower of boxes. The stove and microwave were no longer accessible and the refrigerator had stopped working. The freezer no longer kept things frozen, but kept things cold enough to act as a fridge as long as there was ice in there. So, rather than clearing the space to get the old fridge out and replace it, my parents instead started buying one to two bags of ice per day to keep things cold. At one point, they secured the cash to buy a new fridge, and had even purchased it, but they were unable to get it in the house. The store kept calling, trying to have it delivered. I have no idea how long they held it, but I know they eventually gave up. I hope my parents got their money back. A spare microwave was hooked up in the living room, in the midst of the ever-growing pile.

Food was stored in plastic containers and recycled tubs and jars, to protect it from ants and rodents. Of course there was a persistent mouse problem. Beyond just being disgusting, the sound of scratching and scurrying in the dark while trying to fall asleep was so irritating. I think that was one reason I started keeping my small, loud desk fan on whenever I was home – to drown out sounds like that. (There were also birds in the attic-like space between the ceiling and roof, and I could hear them as well at times.) On two separate occasions – once in the shower, once while I was asleep – I was attacked by Hawai`i's famous "B-52" flying cockroaches. It was *horrifying*. The toilet in the front bathroom stopped working, so all three of us used the one in my parents' half-bathroom (no, that door didn't close either). There was just enough room in the front bathroom to use the shower and sink. The washing machine was also in the front bathroom, by the door that led out to the back porch, and it was slowly becoming less accessible. I don't recall ever washing clothes at home because when it was not blocked by stuff, I was too little to reach everything. I was probably the only kid in the world who wanted to help do laundry…perhaps simply because I could not.

I remember wishing my school had a Home Economics class, so I could learn how to cook. I had helped make bacon once, on vacation at a beach house. I wanted so badly to cook more than bacon. I innocently figured Home Economics would teach you how to do laundry and basically all the other domesticated stuff most people learn at home. (Hey, I knew how to sew, at least!)

I had always kept my room as tidy and clean as possible, purging and reorganizing as much as I could whenever the mood struck. I actually liked cleaning; it was almost a luxury. As a teen, I spent all of my home time in my room. I spent countless hours staring at the ceiling, imagining my dream house. I never had a preference for the size of that house, I just imagined it with space. My bedroom – walls still lined with those metal bookcases – became my world. I did my homework and ate my dinner on my bed. That big, metal desk was still in my room, but there was not enough space for a chair, so when I eventually got a computer, I set it up off to the side, on top of some boxes of who-knows-what that had always been there, and sat ON the desk.

What used to be my bedroom

The closet in my room was always full of my mom's older, nicer clothes, and blocked by a big old rocking chair, so a stand-alone wardrobe for my clothes sat over the foot of my bed. I had to stand up on my bed to get out those clothes. My longer dresses were hung on the corner of one of the old bookcases. I felt so weird for not having a closet like everyone else.

Once I started driving, I spent minimal time at home, keeping busy with extra-curricular activities, a part-time job, and eating nice, home-cooked dinners at my then-boyfriend's parents' house. Eventually, our washing machine broke. Again, it was too much of a hassle to replace it, so we started using a nearby Laundromat. I hated going there; so much time was lost while we waited around, and it was always so uncomfortably warm in there.

Periodically friends would ask why they never saw my house. "My mom is a kind of a pack-rat," I would say, and then quickly change the subject. Or, "Your house is nicer." If I ever caught a ride home from somewhere, I tried to distract the person while I exited the car, so they wouldn't look at my house. A few times, I asked people to drop me off down the street. "Just let me off here," I would say, "that way you don't have to go all the way up the road to turn around," or whatever. They probably thought I was strange, especially when I insisted, but I would die if they saw my house.

People could see enough on the outside anyway. For whatever reason, my parents' property never effectively grew grass, only weeds. My mom loves plants, so she grew all kinds of different trees, bushes, and flowers. There were lots of potted plants, including an orchid as old as me, and I remember the papaya tree in the back, the pomegranate along the side, and aloe in the front. I think their Surinam cherry, coconut, plumeria, and calamansi trees are all still there, along with a ton of other stuff. My mom has always taken pride in her yard, but the weeds have always been a problem – often overgrown. As my parents got older, it became harder to maintain the weeds; they had to rely on neighborhood kids to cut it for them. So even before you saw the house, you saw the "desert jungle" surrounding it. But on the corner of the house, which sits elevated on the corner of a cul-de-sac, is a large picture window. It is one of the first things you see as you approach the house, and you could not miss the mountain of boxes completely blocking it from the inside.

I went off to college in 2001, with every intention of returning home after I graduated. My first winter break, I scrounged together just enough money for a round-trip ticket, packed up all my warm-weather clothes (all the while teasing my roommates who were sticking around on the chilly East Coast), and headed home. I was so homesick and could not wait to see my friends and family. I was also very

Front yard

eager to see the condition of my house. I don't know why, but I thought maybe, just maybe, my mom had cleaned it up a little. I often encouraged her and my dad to try and get rid of stuff, make some room, or at least make sure my room was preserved as I had left it. She always said they were "working on it."

My heart sank as I walked through the door and saw even more stuff than before. I thought the house could not be any more cluttered, but it was. Still, I was happy to be home, and enjoyed my month off. I had missed the heavenly Hawaiian sun and trade winds and the view of the ocean from my parents' property, but there was still no reason or comfortable way to hang out at the house, so I passed most of my time at the beach or out with friends.

I continued to go home for winter breaks for all but one year, and much to my horror and chagrin, the house got worse and worse. Each time I left, I pleaded with my parents to clean up the house so it was nicer when I moved back after college. By the time I graduated, though, there was no room for me left in that house. My dad started sleeping on my bed because my parents' bed was overrun with so much stuff, and my mom slept in a ball on a small patch she had cleared for herself there. I passionately abhorred the prospect of staying in Pennsylvania any longer, but now I had nowhere to stay in Hawai`i. Plus, I had accepted a job right out of college and gotten engaged. I figured I would live and work out here for a while, at least until I could afford my own place in Hawai`i, and then I would move back with my husband.

Parents' bedroom

Beginning of the hallway toward the bedrooms

My homesickness was intense and perpetual, so I resolved to try and go home at least every other year. The year after Billy and I got married, we decided to take our first trip together to Hawai`i. I gave my parents almost a year's notice, so they would have enough time to clean up the house and make room for us. We knew we would be busy seeing sights and friends, so we really just needed a place to sleep and shower. "Oh! OK!" my mom said. I stressed how serious I was. We could not afford a hotel, never mind the absurdity of having to even think about staying anywhere but my parents' house. Whenever I talked to my parents on the phone, I would ask for status updates on the house. "We're working on it," my mom would say. Sigh. I had heard that one before. Finally, a couple of months before our arrival, my parents confessed that their house would not be ready for us, so they were talking to neighbors and people from church about putting us up for the two weeks we would be there. We ended up staying with a very nice man from church with a spare bedroom, who would open his home to us again when we returned two years later.

Whenever we returned, I discovered that the house was disturbingly and unimaginably worse than before. I could barely enter, and I never let Billy go in. With every visit, I climbed, sweating (so much for that breeze), to what used to be my room to retrieve photo albums and jewelry, for fear that the place would one day implode or burn down and I would lose the few material things from my past that I still cared about. I was frustrated and mortified and disgusted. *How can anyone live like this?*

At some point in early 2010, I learned that my mom had moved into my room, sleeping (again, in a ball) on a tiny spot on my tiny bed. My dad was sleeping in the car. He was using portable urinals or public facilities so he did not have to climb to their half-bathroom at the back of the house. I was beyond furious. *How could she do this? How dare she! Why won't Dad speak up and stop this?* To make matters impossibly more dreadful, there was an incident most likely involving arson that nearly caught my parents' house on fire. It was late and they were sleeping when it happened; they barely made it out of there. A kind soul from church had recently repainted their house's exterior. If not for that, the fire surely would have engulfed the house in flames. Thankfully there was no damage, but I had had enough.

I was complaining to a friend for the millionth time about this, to which he said, "Why don't you apply to 'Hoarders' or something?" I had previously explored the possibility of submitting them to "Extreme Makeover Home Edition" but quickly dismissed that idea when I read that submitting a video was part of the application process. How would I get a video, being 5,000 miles away? I did not think it would be worth the trouble, anyway, considering the types of stories that actually make it onto the show. Sure, my mom did a lot for the community in her heyday and was suffering from horrible arthritis, among other things, but they didn't have 15 kids, weren't fostering a zoo of rescued animals, and didn't have any other significant tragedies or sob stories. I had heard of "Hoarders," but not having cable, I had never seen the show. I had also heard of "Clean Sweep" and "Hoarding: Buried Alive," but was even less familiar with them. So I went to A&E's website and checked it out, watching clips of a couple of episodes.

On June 23, 2010, I submitted an application to "Hoarders" with zero expectation of ever hearing back from them.

Driveway / front of car port

Two days later, I received an email from Screaming Flea Productions, confirming receipt of my application and requesting photos of the house. I wrote back, explaining that I was in Pennsylvania, but I would try to figure out a way to get the photos. I thought about begging a friend or cousin to do it while my dad was home but my mom was out; but I figured Mom would not appreciate that, and she would never consent to being on the show if we did anything behind her back.

End of hallway between doorway to parents' bedroom and my bedroom

Instead, I asked her directly if she would be open to the possibility of receiving professional help cleaning up the house at no cost to them. When she said yes, I told her it would be for a TV show on A&E that handles the subject tastefully and sensitively. She was interested. Finally, I told her I needed pictures of the house, but I would send her the money for film, and I would take care of processing it (she didn't/doesn't have a digital camera). With the cash I sent to her, I included a mail-away, postage-paid order envelope to drop the film in when she was done taking the pictures. I gave her one week to complete her task. Although she agreed, I doubted that she would follow through; but lo and behold, not long after her deadline passed, the pictures were developed and in my hands. A friend scanned them for me, and I quickly sent them to my contact at Screaming Flea.

By August 23, 2010, the network had made their decision to include our story on the show, and we would soon be on our way to Hawai`i to begin a very new, unpredictable, exciting adventure that would forever change our lives and the lives of my parents.

I am the daughter of a compulsive hoarder. This is my story.

Chapter 2: Hoarders

I kept this journal during our trip, and for a few of the events that followed the filming of our episode. I anticipated that this would be an experience I would not want to forget!

Sunday, September 19, 2010
Although Billy had to work this morning – in the city, on the day of a Phillies home game – we got to the airport with plenty of time to spare…and thank goodness, because Billy realized as we were checking in our bags that he forgot his wallet at home. (As if I weren't already out-of-my-mind anxious about flying with our 11½-month old for the first time!) Long story short, we are grateful for the selfless friends we have in our life that were able to help us out at the drop of a hat and bring his wallet to us!

Thankfully, we had no problems getting through the security checkpoint. The next challenge was finding someone to switch seats with Billy, because our seats were not together. By the grace of God working through some very kind people willing to swap seats, we were able to sit together after all. So we survived what I thought would be the hard part. Rory did pretty well with the take-off; we used Earplanes, but I also nursed her. She started fussing when she got really tired, and finally fell asleep – just long enough to allow us to eat something, anyway.

The final challenge of the day was catching our connecting flight in Los Angeles, changing airline carriers in less than 2 hours. While that doesn't sound daunting, at LAX, that means going OUTSIDE, waiting for and catching the connection bus that only runs every 5 minutes or so, *and then going through security again*. (This, my friends, is precisely why I NEVER book flights that require changing airlines. It can be a nightmare!) Amazingly there was no line at the security checkpoint; but by the time we reached our gate, I barely had enough time to change Rory's diaper. When we were done, they were already boarding. I had to go ahead of Billy, who was trying to get us something to eat in the terminal. I will spare you the painful details that follow; suffice to say I was a very unhappy ball of stress. Looking at the big picture, though, we made our flight, and at least this time, we were already seated together.

For the record, I have never been a fan of the original airline that shall remain nameless, but since we didn't pay for this trip, we really had no choice. Would you believe there was no in-flight entertainment or complimentary snacks? No peanuts, pretzels, nothing! Both were present in abundance on our second flight, with Delta. The Delta crew also seemed friendlier.

Once we were in the air, our flight from LAX to HNL was so much better. Rory slept, I slept, and we got there safely, WITH OUR BAGS. In fact, for the first time in my life, our bags were the first to come out on to the belt. Mom greeted us at baggage claim, we took the shuttle to our car rental where Dad met us, we picked up our rental car, and were on our way to the hotel. We're staying at the Aqua Waikiki Wave – a nice little place; nothing fancy, but decent. Rory went right down with no problem, and Billy and I turned in around midnight. What a long day... Not the smoothest start to a trip, but we made it, and I am home!

Monday, September 20, 2010
Rory woke up at 1:30am (she is still on East Coast time). I nursed her and, thankfully, she fell back asleep until about 3am. We went to Walmart around 7am to get some essentials and then grabbed some breakfast. When we got back to the hotel, we were informed that we were being upgraded to a suite.

Upon checking in on our first night, we were asked for a credit card and told that only the first night had been paid for. I was made aware of this when I called to confirm our stay, but was told to ask about it when we arrived; so I did, but no one at the front desk seemed to have any knowledge of alternative payment arrangements, etc. I called our contact at Screaming Flea, who contacted the hotel to straighten things out, and I guess this was their way of apologizing for the inconvenience. At first we debated the necessity of an upgrade, but we would have been foolish to not accept. The room was twice the size, had an ocean view, and Rory got her own room! After we moved all our stuff (which took forever because only one elevator was working), we finally made our way to the beach, which was just a short walk away. Rory loved the ocean! She giggled every time I jumped with her in the waves, and was absolutely fascinated by the sand.

After we got back and cleaned up, my parents arrived and stayed with Rory as she napped for over two hours – finally, a real nap! Billy and I snuck out for lunch at the International Marketplace and browsed through the shops. When we got back, we actually had to wake up Rory from her nap; you could tell she was disoriented, thinking she had been down for the night. She was really fussy – combination of jetlag, a cold, and teething – so we went for a walk, which helped a little bit. Thankfully she did fine at our dinner at Zippy's with my high school buddies, quietly enjoying a bowl of shredded cheese and a dinner roll. Upon our return to the hotel, we were greeted unexpectedly by my cousin and aunty – a nice surprise! I bathed Rory while Billy helped my dad with a flat tire, then I put Rory down, and we all hung out for a bit. Once everyone left, Billy and I went to bed at 9:30pm; we were exhausted, and needed the sleep SO badly.

Tuesday, September 21, 2010
Rory woke us up at 4am…still early, but we're getting there. She's doing a LOT better now that she's semi-adjusted, and getting over her cold. I think the sunshine is helping, too. Right after breakfast, we went to the beach again. It was so nice get there before the crowds; I'd never seen Waikiki Beach so deserted! After the beach, we changed and walked down to the Honolulu Zoo. Rory loved the elephants and giraffes and the baby goats in the petting zoo. She fell asleep on the long walk back to the International Marketplace, via Kalakaua Avenue, where we grabbed lunch again and then returned again later for a little souvenir shopping. (I've always loved that place! Though it's hopping late at night on weekends, and noisy all day, it's actually really great staying just a few stories above it. It will probably never be this conveniently accessible to us again. I took advantage of it!)

Filming commenced this morning at my parents' house – "a day in the life" of my mom and dad. It was a long day for my mom, but she reportedly remained in good spirits for most of it. The crew got their first taste of her "controlling perfectionism," though, when they accidentally knocked down a pile of stuff and she flipped out. I don't think they knew what they were in for…

We wrapped up our day by hitting Walmart again, then walked across the street to the Likelike Drive-in to meet my cousin for dinner. I don't know why I can't remember ever eating at that iconic restaurant; the food was delicious! I brought my leftovers back for my dad, as I know he appreciates a free hot meal these days.

Wednesday, September 22, 2010
Rory finally slept past 6am! After breakfast, we headed down to the Board Room of the hotel where we were to meet the producer for our interviews. We were there at 8am on the dot, but everyone else, including my dad, was running late. Meanwhile, Billy and I met Matt Paxton, the professional organizer in charge of the clean-up that starts tomorrow. He told us about himself, how he got into the business, and shared some stories of past hoarders, then he gave us a helpful pep talk.

We finally got started around 9:15am – my dad went first, then me, then Billy. We had a second room across the hall to hang out in while we waited our turn. Thankfully, Rory took a nice, long nap during my interview, leaving less work for Daddy and Grandpa!

Burt, the producer; Kevin, the audio man; and Joaquin, the camera man – these were the guys who did our interviews. They were amazing gentlemen, professional but fun, and so patient and easygoing. I felt completely comfortable doing my interview with them. Of course, I broke out a little on my face due to the stress of traveling, so I felt very self-conscious the entire time. The air conditioning had to be turned off while filming to avoid even the slightest background noise, so it started to get hot in the room, especially with the bright lights. There were several occasions during which I had to repeat an answer to a question because of a bus, helicopter, truck backing up, siren, or other outside noise. I was beyond thankful I was not by myself with Rory during all of this; I wouldn't have been able to keep her quiet long enough if she had had to stay in the same room as me! I NEVER take Billy or our families for granted.

After my interview, I met my dad back upstairs in our hotel room, gave him those leftovers, which he enjoyed, and then talked on the phone with Dr. Suzanne Chabaud, the psychiatrist who would be working with us on-set. I gave her some insight about my mom, myself, my childhood, etc. She said she is very interested in studying the effects of hoarding on the children of a hoarder; I told her I would be open to speaking with her further in the future.

We stopped by my parents' house in the late afternoon, expecting to walk through for the cameras, but they were still busy with my mom, so we hung out with my dad, then Billy and I took a walk around the block with Rory. My old neighborhood looks so different through my adult eyes…yet somehow, still the same. I was flooded with so many vivid memories. We met up with my parents for dinner (where I only had a chance to eat half of my dinner because it was SO late and Rory was well past her bedtime; things ran later than expected at their house), then headed back to the hotel.

Thursday, September 23, 2010
Another full night of sleep, praise the Lord! Today began the clean-up of the house. We ate breakfast and dropped off Rory at my parents' friend's house, where she stayed for the day. We all got acquainted (we met the psychiatrist, the other producer and camera/audio crew, and the clean-up team); then, while the crews got set up, we ran down to Home Depot to see if we could work out a deal on some new appliances for my parents, which we wanted to be ready to give them if

they made the space for them. We got contact information for the manager who had the authority for this but wasn't there at the moment, I called our contact at Screaming Flea and passed the info along (so she could send a letter to the manager verifying that my parents were really going to be on the show, etc.), and then we ran a quick personal errand before going back to the house.

Billy and I got "miked up" on arrival and were instructed to be ourselves, even if they could hear every word coming out of our mouths. We were to take/make phone calls as normal, talk amongst ourselves, jump into conversations on camera, etc. True reality TV! Once in a while, we'd have fun with the crew, saying super-silly stuff that only they could hear just to make them laugh.

Before we tackled the cleaning, we had a group chat with Matt, then they wanted to catch Billy's and my reaction to the house's condition…so we entered the house. Wow. I did not think it would be possible for it to get worse than it was the last time I'd seen it. Even Matt said it was the worst he had ever seen, in terms of the sheer *volume*! This was going to be tougher than I thought.

Finally, the clean-up began. It got off to an extremely slow start. My mom wanted to have a say in every single thing, so Matt's initial strategy was to have items brought out to her and she would determine on the spot whether to keep or discard them. This proved to not work, however, and even though we were letting my mom stay in control, she got frustrated. There was too much talking and rationalizing, and not enough action. In three hours, they had gotten through only about THREE FEET of stuff!

We broke for lunch around 1pm. Billy felt we needed to leave to give us a break, so we went to Jack in the Box. I took one of the plate lunches provided to us and brought it with us, while he actually ate there. As we were leaving, Billy called a friend at our church back in PA, who put us on speakerphone and prayed for us with the youth group. On our way back to my parents' house, I suggested stopping at their church to see if we could catch their pastor and have him pray with us, too. Unfortunately he wasn't there, but it was nice to see the outside of their new building, and run into my old preschool teacher!

We reconvened after lunch, and jumped right back into everything. Just a few minutes into it, my mom got very distressed because she was feeling pressured to get rid of everything, so they started bringing out multiple things at once and letting her sift through everything on her own without the guidance of Matt or Dr. Chabaud. Eventually, they confronted my mom about the fact that she was merely organizing and re-boxing all of her stuff and not getting rid of anything, which was only contributing to her hoarding and not helping overcome it. Multiple times she was asked why we were all even there, since she wasn't accepting anyone's help. The clean-up crew was literally just standing around, and they even sent back one of the trucks and a couple of guys because they were not needed. Finally she had a breakdown where she started blaming everyone, especially her deceased parents and siblings; she never felt appreciated, loved, secure. Her behavior was embarrassing, childish, and pathetic; but it was healthy and extremely necessary, and a normal part of the healing process. We let her vent then reassured her that we loved her and were proud of her for letting this happen even though she didn't want to, etc.

By the end of today, only a few feet of the living room got cleared...but it was a start. We met up for dinner with one of my friends, which was fun, and bought some pie to go. My parents met us back at our hotel so they could eat dinner and take a shower. After my shower, I sat down with my pie, and said to my mother, "Mom, I just need to say two things: First, we are very proud of you. Second, I want you to utilize the help you guys are being provided with while they are here, because we only have one more day." Or something like that...but it was apparently encouraging enough to get her to open up and talk about her experience for the day! Billy then chimed in and said his piece. Mom was receptive and positive, and even told us that she and Dad had committed to cleaning the house on their own for two hours every day after this was all over. Obviously prayers were being answered here, and we were making progress with her after all. We had such a great visit together, and ended the evening on very good terms.

Friday, September 24, 2010
Today started much like yesterday, but we got a late start with the clean-up because of my mom – who, by the way, admitted out loud to the psychiatrist when she came outside, "I really do have problems." Well, good for Mom for acknowledging that on her own!

The clean-up started where we left off, and gained some momentum when Matt instructed the clean-up crew to take nine obviously-useless things (i.e. empty boxes) directly to the dumpster and only show my mom one thing to decide upon. This was kind of working, until my mom started feeling "pressured" again. It was time for serious confrontation, during which Matt revealed that he was hoping to surprise them with a new bed if he could, but if more wasn't cleaned out, he was going to cancel the order – and he had until Noon. I don't know if that information made a difference, but I am certain it motivated my dad, who has been unfairly sleeping in the car for several months...

Billy was now helping direct the clean-up crew, while coaxing and urging my mom to allow them to be more liberal with the things that were really OK to throw out. It all came to a head when Billy approached my mom and asked her to trust us with making the decisions for her. She needed to let go of anything, for example, that was completely destroyed by rodents and/or moisture, or way past expiration. Everyone was on high alert for certain items that she was looking for, including my baby book, her wedding album, and some cash and jewelry. Of those items, only my baby book was located, but even that one find seemed to be enough to encourage and excite her to keep going. At the end of the day, she was disappointed that the other things were never found, and is convinced that they were thrown out, but the important thing was what was accomplished: the living room was cleared out and they got that bed. My dad would not be sleeping in his car tonight!

Unfortunately, by the time we were done, I felt too ill to enjoy that success. I was not sure whether it was dehydration or sun stroke or some kind of bug, but nothing eased it. My stomach ached SO badly. We went back to the hotel, put Rory down, I showered, then TRIED to eat…but couldn't, so I just went to bed. My parents came over to the hotel again, but I was practically asleep by then. I do know my mom had created a list of everything she couldn't find, which was upsetting her, but Billy kept her reasonable and calm enough to be able to talk to both of them. I do remember this: as they were leaving, my mom kissed me and said, "Thank you." I think I responded, "Thank you, we're proud of you."

Saturday, September 25, 2010
This ended up being a day of rest, though not by choice. I still felt sick, so I stayed in bed half the day and ventured out just long enough to get some sunlight and grab some very basic sushi. We also bumped into Matt who was getting ready to fly out, and told him about the list my mom had compiled. He said that's normal, and continued to encourage us. I wish we could have had another hour with him, just picking his brain about everything!

In the afternoon my parents came over to visit with us one last time. They really enjoyed seeing Rory, and I know they're going to miss her so much. My dad helped Billy load the car, and then we parted ways. I hope we see a lot more of them soon, and I hope that house gets cleaned up.

We dropped off the rental car and made it to the airport with plenty of time to spare. Our seats were separated again on our red-eye to San Francisco (totally separated this time; we were each in different rows), but thankfully Delta was able to reassign our seats so we didn't have to negotiate with three rows of people at 10pm. Rory had fallen asleep on the way to the airport, but woke up as we were checking in. Thankfully she fell back asleep once we were in the air, and slept for most of that flight. She slept again for a couple of hours from SFO to PHL. The flights themselves were fine, and I was slowly feeling better, but still not great. Needless to say, I was relieved when we landed, claimed our luggage with no problems, and were on our way to our own house. I was surprisingly glad to be back. Happy as I was to be home in Hawai`i, and as memorable and life-changing as this trip was for everyone, we had our share of exhausting challenges that detracted from whatever leisure we had. Here's hoping it was all worth it…

October 2010
A couple days after we returned to PA, my dad informed us that my mother had become very upset about the outcome of the clean-up, and advised us to not call her for a few days. We complied. We informed him that we had a new fridge on standby for them, as our gift, if they would clean up the kitchen. That was their next goal.

On 10/6 – Aurora's first birthday – we received a package in the mail from my mother, containing a blanket that she had crocheted for Rory (that she had included with all the stuff we were using/borrowing from them during our visit in September). Enclosed with the blanket was a terse note that detailed how to care for it, how long it took her to make it, when she started making it, and finally, "Since you left it behind, I guess you didn't want it? If you don't want it, just toss it out or give away." Honestly, I did not know that she was GIVING it to us at the time, or that it was even made for Rory! She was clearly angry when she scribbled the note, but her pitiful attitude was maddening. I resented her for taking the attention off my daughter's special day, and selfishly putting it all back on herself. I called Dad and asked him to please thank her for us, but also let her know that her mindset was wrong and I did not appreciate the note.

On 10/13, I called my mom to check on her, and see how she was doing after having water removed from her knee. She was OK but in a lot of pain. Then I made the mistake of asking about the house. She unleashed all her pent-up negativity in response to the clean-up process, stating that she felt betrayed and couldn't trust anyone, completely disregarding the good intentions of it all, and the fact that we were doing this FOR HER.

"Did Dad tell you I couldn't even sleep on that bed for the first couple nights?" she asked.
"Why?"
"You got that bed for HIM."
"No… Seriously?"

"Did you know after they hauled away that dumpster (that she had climbed into to try and retrieve stuff – which Matt warned us she would probably do), I sat on the curb and cried for two hours, with my pain pills in my hand? I was gonna just take them all."

She went on and on about how we don't care about her, I'm so heartless, she can't believe I'm her daughter and that I could be so cold about the whole thing. She said she would be bitter about this for the rest of her life.

I was at work during this call, so I couldn't react the way she wanted and loudly demonstrate the explosive emotions I was actually feeling inside, and my composure obviously frustrated her even more. I did say, calmly, that I couldn't believe how selfish she was acting, and how unfortunate it was that she couldn't just appreciate our help and sacrifices. I said I was sorry she felt betrayed, but I hope she eventually realizes this was done out of love, and it was meant for the best. I added that I would not be speaking with her again until she calmed down. The call ended with her basically threatening to kill herself, so I called Dad to let him know she was being crazy, and make sure she didn't do anything stupid – even though I figured this was all just for attention and pity, which I wasn't going to give her. I knew she wouldn't kill herself, but I was still relieved that she didn't.

November 2010
11/25 – I had received a message from Screaming Flea that our episode would be airing on Monday night, so I called my parents to let them know, and to wish them both a Happy Thanksgiving. This was the first time I'd spoken with Mom in over a month. She was brief but calmer, though she did demand a copy of all 30+ hours of video footage we had shot. I reminded her that we all signed a release that made all footage the property of Screaming Flea, and that they would never honor such a request, nor are they obligated to do so, so I'm not asking them for it. Her reason for the demand was, "I know you guys were scheming behind my back and I want to hear everything that was said." She also asked why she didn't get to view the footage before airing. I explained that that's not how it works, but I would send them their DVD copy of the episode as soon as we received them.

On 11/29, our episode aired. We didn't have cable, so we watched at a friend's house (cringing at the close-ups). A lot of important pieces were cut out, but we felt they did a great job portraying our situation as accurately and tastefully as possible. I made sure my parents had their DVD copy in their hands as soon as possible, since they were unable to watch it live. Mom had little to say in response. We took that as a good sign.

Billy visited the "Hoarders" message board on A&E's website to see what kind of feedback people were leaving about our story. I felt it would be best for me to not look, but I let him share some highlights. There were a lot of mixed reviews. Everyone felt bad for my dad for sleeping in the car; most people commented on the selfishness of my mother; some people were confused about why she hoarded, while still others questioned why my dad and I didn't do anything about it. One person apparently knew us personally, and left a lot of praise and encouragement for us. Overall it was evident that the general public is ignorant about the disorder, which sparked an interest in both Billy and me to learn more in order to understand it – if nothing else, to continue helping my mom.

(Little did I know how much I was about to learn!)

December 2010
On 12/19, we purchased the refrigerator for my parents, from the Home Depot down the road from them. We had been in touch with the manager since September, and he was ready whenever we were to give us a discount and help in any other way he could.

My parents worked hard to continue cleaning on their own. They utilized their aftercare budget for the service of two professional organizers over the course of a couple weeks. Our Aftercare Coordinator called us with occasional reports, and though my mom was stubborn and difficult to work with, they at least got the ball moving and cleared enough space to get the old, broken fridge out. The new fridge wasn't delivered right away (my Dad said they needed "a few more days"), but when they finally got it, they were grateful. We sent them a grocery gift card for Christmas, so they could fill the fridge with the types of food they hadn't been able to keep at home in over a decade. No more bags of ice to keep stuff cold! We prayed they would keep it in clean, working order.

March 2011
We got a call from our contact at Screaming Flea, informing us that A&E wanted to do a follow-up episode that would include our story, and they would fly us back. We called my parents, who agreed without hesitation. My mom's immediate motivation was to air her grievances and demand recompense. I told her that that was not the purpose of this, and if she didn't cooperate, they wouldn't do the show. She understood, but still had things to get off her chest. Fine. We booked the shoot for the beginning of April, but didn't tell them we would be coming. We didn't want to influence their participation in any way, and also just wanted to have a little fun surprising them.

April 2011

We arrived in HNL on 4/1, and arranged a surprise dinner with the help of my cousin. My parents weren't expecting it at all, and they were both genuinely excited to see us. We made the difficult decision to not bring Rory this time because it was a very short trip (she would not have time to adjust to the time difference). We enjoyed our meal with them, and then turned in at the Makaha Resort. We figured staying on the West side of the island this time would allow us to spend more time with my parents, than if we'd stayed in Waikiki again. It was a nice change.

On 4/2, the small crew (Joaquin was back) filmed my parents at home in the morning, and then we visited the house and they captured our reaction to the house's current condition. I was relieved but disappointed. It was better, but still not good. They still had a very LONG way to go...but their new bed was still clear, and the fridge was still accessible. They could get to the back doors now. The whole kitchen needs to be redone at some point, and the bathrooms are still hard to get to, but at least they had SOME living space now. My mom did air some of her grievances, but she kept it short and to the point. I think it helped her to vent a little bit, so everyone let her say what she needed to. We were done by lunchtime, so we enjoyed a leisurely day on the West side. My parents had remarked earlier that they only had one set of sheets for the new bed, so we bought them another set at K-Mart...followed by Leonard's malasadas, of course.

On 4/3, we did our individual interviews at the Aqua Waikiki Wave (where we'd stayed back in September). We were done by lunchtime again, so we enjoyed some time together at the International Marketplace, and then took my parents to the North Shore for some Matsumoto's shave ice. My mother who had lived on O'ahu for nearly 67 years claimed she'd never had it (!), so it was cute to see her enjoy it like a kid. We had a nice time with them.

On 4/4, we relaxed and grabbed a bite with my parents before we had to leave. The trip was much too short, but it was NICE. My mom was a completely different person – happier than I had seen her in a very, very long time. She was rested and calm. Free, almost. We loved our visit, and so did they. *Yes, it was worth it. All of it.*

June 2011

We took a family vacation with Billy's sisters and parents and a couple of friends of theirs, which we had planned before "Hoarders" happened. We all rented a big beach house in Hau'ula, which was about 45 minutes from my parents' house. I was busy with my 10-year high school reunion and doing some touristy stuff with the family, and we had Rory with us again, so we didn't spend much time with my parents; but we did have a couple of meals with them, got to go to church with them, and we did visit them at home. No change since April, for better or worse, but that bed was still clear – and Mom still seemed happy. She was healing.

Chapter 3: Hoarding Hurts

"Pay special attention to anything you try to hide." – Gretchen Rubin

* * *

When you think about how hoarding affects the child of a hoarder, what comes to mind? It is natural to assume one of two extreme outcomes: the child becomes a hoarder, or the child becomes a neat freak. These are merely superficial effects. Seldom do people realize the mental and emotional detriment hoarding can have on the ones growing up amongst the "stuff."

My motivation to finally seek therapy initially had nothing to do with my childhood experiences, my mother's hoarding, or the filming of our "Hoarders" episode. In fact, I had spent the past ten years questioning what was wrong with ME. I would often remark, "My parents are still alive and together, I have a good relationship with both of them, and I had a great childhood full of fond memories. Good schooling, lots of traveling, year after year of cool birthday parties at all the popular spots, fun with friends… I don't know why I am always so angry or over-sensitive."

I was about sixteen years old when I first recognized that I had an issue with anger. I was not violent or abusive, and I did not act out behaviorally – I was an honor student, rarely got into trouble, never touched drugs or alcohol – but I was constantly irate and easily offended. Yeah, I was also a teenager. But something just wasn't right. I sought the guidance of our school chaplain, who tried to help me uncover the source of my negative emotions, but I was clueless. In the end, all he could do was pray with me.

In college, I reached another breaking point that drove me to see the on-campus counselor. This time, I wasn't angry, I was just confused. I was in a toxic, emotionally-abusive relationship that constantly made me feel worthless and guilty, but before we could even touch on that subject, she wanted to get to know me.

After two sessions she unofficially diagnosed me with Obsessive Compulsive Disorder, which was not at all a surprise. We primarily focused on my obsessions, which, at the time, included my fixation on the musical *Phantom of the Opera* and other fantastical worlds. She told me I was likely obsessing over fantasy to escape from reality. I don't remember how many sessions I had with her, or much else of what we discussed, but these things were profound to me and made sense. OK, I wasn't going crazy. My problem has a name. I was still stuck in that awful relationship, but at least I knew a little more about myself.

This was not the first time I was hearing about OCD. In high school, I had taken an intro to psychology course, and even then I felt I could identify with the disorder; but it takes on a whole different meaning when you start understanding it in the context of your own behavior and thoughts.

A few years ago, I got fed up with myself again. I was losing my temper quickly and constantly and taking everything way too personally. In retrospect, I believe the birth control pill I was taking at the time was adversely contributing to my overall moodiness, but I had no idea at the time. I was pissed off at everyone, but I was even more pissed that I was letting myself be affected or offended by every little thing. This time I sought the help of one of our pastors. He related to me, but in that initial meeting, could not help me beyond praying with me. He warned that anger was a "generational sin," shared his own personal experiences with it, and suggested reaching out to a professional therapist. But I was convinced I could figure this out and overcome it on my own. I prayed about it, of course, but not consistently, so I never made any progress.

I was back in his office about a year later (early 2011), about a completely different issue. After pouring out my heart, he started associating my problems with my mother's hoarding. I never would have made those connections on my own, and the profoundness of his analysis switched on something inside me that helped me see everything in a completely different light. It excited me! I had failed to make the most important connection that was right in front of me all along. It was always easy to see the obvious, superficial effects my mother's hoarding had on me: I was overly organized, I hated clutter and chaos, etc. But this! It felt like a thousand light bulbs turned on in my head.

Still, after two meetings with him, he once again recommended professional help. I held on to that advice, but did not act upon it. Instead, I prayed more. I meditated on some Bible verses that both encouraged and challenged me to keep my head in the right place. I took up martial arts to help me feel better physically and improve my focus and discipline. I picked up the phone to confide in friends when I was feeling down, even if it was just to ask for their prayers and support.

In August 2011, for reasons I may never be able to identify or explain, I started feeling very down. I felt invisible and worthless. The weeks between August and September fell into one of the darkest points in my life, emotionally. I was not overly public about it, though my Facebook statuses were a bit gloomy. It was pretty obvious to anyone paying attention that I was bumming hard about something, but that just made things worse because I was simply not getting the kinds of responses I wanted. I figured SOMEONE would notice and say SOMETHING. I started resenting everyone for ignoring me on Facebook. The negative self-talk that cycled in my head was something like this:

> *OK, maybe they aren't intentionally "ignoring" me...but they certainly aren't acknowledging my cries for help. Really, I just need some encouragement. A virtual hug. A simple reminder that they haven't forgotten about me. That I matter. I want attention, and don't know how else to ask for it. But people aren't commenting. They obviously didn't care. Screw them all. I ALWAYS leave them a word of encouragement, or just tell them I'm praying for them. And of course what's-her-face has nothing to say to me. She only pays attention to the stupid, shallow, silly stuff I put up there – never anything of consequence. We were never really friends anyway. Seriously, though, how can she not care at all? If people care, they should respond. I'm tired of hearing, "People don't know what to say." Aren't they my friends? And if so-and-so just puts up a sad face, she gets ten comments in an hour – some from mutual friends – "Aww, what's wrong?" or "Hugs!" Makes no sense. I GIVE UP. I need new friends. I need to get the hell out of here.*

And so on, and so on, for weeks. Then, out of the blue, someone would write on my Wall or send me a kind text message, and I would be OK again, at least for a few days. Then it would start all over again. I tried to keep track of the days I felt lowest, to see if there was any pattern or correlation to anything (PMS?), but I saw none. I just recognized the miserable cycle of ups and downs, and could not figure out what was happening to me. My home life and job were above satisfactory, our health was intact, finances were stable. I had a decent life. I had no reason to complain...except, of course, that I felt like all my friends simultaneously disregarded me, or they just did not care about anything I said or did. Why I suddenly slipped into that mindset or why that even started to matter so intensely to me, I still do not know. Perhaps it was because a close friend of mine started getting closer with other friends at that time, and I interpreted our increasing distance as a bad thing, like he was getting bored with me. And of course, I nagged him for reassurance that this wasn't the case...which annoyed him. But our friendship endured through that rough patch, which suggested that this was all in my head.

Out of desperation, I called the aforementioned pastor's wife who was kind of like a wise big sister-type friend. She is brutally honest in an edifying way, is gifted in her way with words, and she always tells you exactly what you need to hear. I needed that, and she was ever-so-gracious to lend me an ear. She already knew a lot about me, my past, and some of my recent interpersonal struggles, so I didn't really have to catch her up on anything. I just told her what was getting me down and emphasized how much I hated feeling this way. I had a pretty good life, so WHAT WAS WRONG WITH ME? She built me up with a lot of positive feedback and validation, listened to and acknowledged my doubts and fears (namely, failure and rejection), and eventually exhorted me to seek that same professional guidance I had been resisting all along.

Within a couple of days, I surrendered. I stopped making excuses for not seeing a therapist. I kept saying that therapy would be the last resort. Well, nothing else was working, so it was time to give it a try. My first appointment was scheduled for September 20, 2011. *It was time to get better.*

I shared my decision to begin therapy with a few close friends, who were nothing but supportive and encouraging. One of them said that I might not click with the very first therapist I meet, but advised me to be persistent until I find a good fit. I knew I would not have any problem opening up, and was determined to tell her my life story in the first fifteen minutes, to get the most out of our session. If it turned out I didn't like her, I wanted to figure that out right away, so as to not waste my time or money. From the very start I appreciated my therapist's style – active listening with helpful feedback and suggestions – and her overall personality and demeanor. She wasn't boring, quiet, or overly empathetic. She was tough with me in a useful and positive way. She gave it to me straight and helped me answer my own questions. She did not hold back where correction was warranted, or when she disagreed. She was exactly the kind of therapist I needed, and I knew immediately that it was a good fit. Even better, I had told her that we were on "Hoarders," and *it just so happened* that she caught a rerun of our episode before our second session. Call it Serendipity or a God Thing, I was elated to hear that. How much better was she then able to *truly* comprehend the severity of my situation, now having a visual aid to support the images I had started creating in her head! It probably saved us the equivalent of two sessions, which excited me because that meant less time explaining, and more time healing.

After my first session, I was hooked. I looked forward to every single meeting after that.

Interestingly, I did not initiate my treatment because I was the daughter of a hoarder. I did not walk in all angry at my parents or troubled by a lost childhood. I wasn't thinking about that at all. When asked why I was there, I said it was to deal with my anger, obsessions, and certain dysfunctional relationships. But like all effective therapists do, she asked about my parents and my childhood, and I told her everything. Once she knew the circumstances in which I grew up, her focus shifted to that. And just as my pastor had done, she quickly connected my issues to the hoarding.

As it turned out, EVERYTHING ever "wrong" with me was and is connected to the hoarding.

One of the earliest exercises my therapist assigned to me was journaling. First, I was to record all of my ongoing negative thoughts – feeling left out of things, feeling rejected/worthless, feeling inadequate, frustration with people's lack of response – and list specific examples. Then I was to list every instance in which I got angry with or offended by someone. That helped identify patterns. Then we took a deeper dive. I was to recall aspects of my parents' house and interactions with me, and figure out how each aspect affected me. This helped identify the link between the hoarding and my current psychological/relational state. So I started digging. Simultaneously, I spent some time researching the effects of hoarding at childrenofhoarders.com, a website I was referred to by Dr. Suzanne Chabaud, who was on "Hoarders" with us. I spent the first two hours of my research with my jaw hanging open, stunned at the parallels of my childhood to those of the other readers and contributors on the site. Everything was becoming clear, and for the first time in my life, I started making sense of the chaos in my head.

The following journal entry was perhaps the strongest breakthrough I have had to date, and is what inspired me to write this book. Here are the connections I made, in no particular order.

> Mom would regularly talk about home renovations, building a deck, cleaning up the kitchen, etc. One Christmas, she even gave me a cookie cookbook. I remember blankly looking at it, wondering what I would ever do with it, then slowly feeling hope rise within me. I felt my eyes light up and my heart flutter as I asked, "Does this mean…? Are we going to clean the kitchen?" Yes. Hopefully soon. The answer was always positive. But never fulfilled. There were many conversations like this.
>
> *Empty promises of cleaning the house or a particular room → Hopes raised high, then dashed → Disappointment → Distrust, cynicism, pessimism*
>
> There were many, many, many arguments, tears, and guilt-trips between Mom and me over the state of my parents' house. As I got older, I became less tolerant and more vocal about it. I was often reprimanded by my parents for being disrespectful or "too critical." I constantly pressured Mom to clean up. Her response was always an irritable "I KNOW," and was usually followed by "I can't get any help around here!" Once in a while, I'd catch her in a good mood, and she would start talking about this project or that plan to start cleaning and organizing her clutter. But it almost always ended with her throwing a temper tantrum because I would keep pushing and pushing until I aggravated her. At that point, Dad would step in and tell me to leave Mom alone and stop upsetting her.
>
> *Dad enabled Mom → Dad disregarded my feelings → My feelings were invalidated → Constant need for affirmation and validation*

No matter how upset I got, or how much I pleaded for the benefit of everyone, Mom would not change or throw stuff out. Sure, I went to a good private school, went on fun vacations with them to Disneyland, Las Vegas, and the neighbor islands. Sure, I had my own car when I turned sixteen. Sure, I basically did whatever I wanted to do. My parents trusted me completely, and never questioned the company I kept or the boys I was interested in – not that they ever had a reason to, as I was a pretty good kid and always kept up my grades. But looking back, it was as if they were overcompensating for a crucial part of every child's life, which I was severely lacking: a safe and nurturing home life.

Mom valued her stuff more than me (and Dad) → Substituted a healthy home life with time spent outside the home → Lack of well-balanced nurturing → Emotional needs neglected → Excessive need for attention and validation (but the inability to ask for it) → Low self-esteem

Affect of the hoard on Mom: high stress and anxiety because of stuff always falling down, or her not being able to find something → Her emotional breakdowns and crippling indecision → Her unpredictable moods → Confusion (especially as a child) → Always waiting on her, did not want to talk to her or be around/with her → Walking on eggshells with everyone for fear of ever offending them

Also…

Mom seemed to hate the situation, but could not change. This was also highly confusing and illogical. As a child I could not come to this realization, but now I understand why I require things to make logical sense. I often need to know why or how something is the way it is.

My inability to control the situation or my mom → Helplessness → Chaos → My desire/need to be or at least feel like I am in control as much as possible → Stubbornness → Inflexibility (i.e. when plans change); possessiveness; overall control issues

Our family (especially Mom) frequently dressing up to fine-dine out or for special occasions → Knowing it was a façade → Intolerance to hypocrisy → Judgmental

Clutter and condition of house itself → Endless daydreaming about an organized house → Idealism → Discontentment → Comparing everything, including relationships

I was severely embarrassed and ashamed of living in that house. Few people had any idea how bad it really was, and it was something we never talked about in public. It was a sore subject for Mom amongst her close relatives, and for me, it was just humiliating. And lonely. I could never have friends over, and we could never host parties or entertain guests. Sometimes I would ask friends to drop me off down the street, so they didn't know which house was mine. And I would NEVER answer the door. When someone knocked while I was home alone, I would literally hide so they could not see I was home, and stay silent until I knew they'd left (this is often defined amongst children of hoarders as "doorbell dread").

Shame → Secret lifestyle → Isolation → Need for acceptance → Overeager to please or impress others (especially when people come into my home); very – sometimes too – open about my personal life and issues with whomever will listen

Frequently, Mom would go through my trash and retrieve things she thought still had use or value. This infuriated me. First of all, although I had nothing to hide, as an insecure teenager, I felt she was violating my privacy. It was bad enough that the door to my bedroom was a screen door that you could barely close due to all the junk in the hallway, and the bathroom door never closed for as long as I can remember. No privacy, ever. Secondly, it was TRASH. It was not meant to be kept. It got to the point where I had to start destroying everything I threw away, so she could not find any use for it. I would rip up paper into tiny pieces, or cut up cardboard boxes and paper cups/plates. Sometimes I would just wait until trash day and take everything out at the last possible minute. Sometimes – especially when I was home during summer breaks – I would do that with her stuff, too. It never made a dent in the hoard, but for me it was a tiny victory. I'd get a rush when the trash truck drove off, and then I would breathe a sigh of relief that I actually got rid of trash. (For the record, she never noticed that the junk was gone.)

The stuff was more important to Mom than respecting my privacy → My feelings were disregarded

Also…

At home, my bedroom was literally my world. There was nowhere else to sit. But even my own room wasn't really mine because it never stopped being the library. I had bookcases as "walls."

Nothing felt like it really belonged to me → Treasure anything I can claim as my own (including relationships) beyond what is normal or healthy → Possessive

Who would have ever thought so many connections could be made? I had no idea, but I wanted to know more. This was just the beginning. It is my hope that sharing these experiences and their psychological effects might help others who have grown up in similar circumstances – and even those who have not.

Chapter 4: Sessions

"I am not a product of my circumstances. I am a product of my decisions."
– Stephen R. Covey

* * *

Once we had established a salient connection to my mother's hoarding, I experienced breakthrough after breakthrough with each successive therapy session.

Although I had a very long journey ahead, the awareness alone lifted the heavy burden of doubt and despair that had been clouding my judgment and perspective all these years. I saw everything with greater clarity and tolerance. I felt myself "getting better," my mind more at ease – far from perfect, but finally on the right path. I was determined to not let the unpleasant pieces of my past ruin my future, my family, or my children. I would keep learning and growing, being careful to identify the origin of my issues without blaming my parents or making excuses for my reactions to things. I am an adult now, I am responsible for my own actions, regardless of my past; and although it certainly shaped a significant part of who I have become, I resolved from the beginning to never resent either of my parents, and to never say, "It's my parents' fault that I'm like this."

Response became an integral piece in understanding my need for validation. The response itself as well as the way it was delivered was important, but not nearly as important as getting a response, period. I entered the business world straight out of college, and quickly learned the necessity of replying to emails and voicemails within one business day. It was expected in that world, but I just considered it a common courtesy. I got so used to operating with such promptness that I started to get more and more impatient communicating in my personal life. I could understand not receiving quick reply to an email because very few of my friends sat in front of a computer all day like I did. I was usually OK, as long as people replied within a week, but if I left a voicemail for a friend and heard nothing back within two days, I immediately jumped to some pessimistic conclusion, like he or she was avoiding me, even if I had not talked to the person in months, and certainly had not said or done anything to warrant such unconstructive thinking. This bled into social networking as I got immersed into MySpace and then Facebook, and also when I started texting. It usually turned out that the person had a valid explanation for not responding immediately, but I continued to assume the worst.

Sometimes when I did get a response, that was really all I required – just a simple acknowledgment to know the message was received (this is especially the case for text messages). Most of the time, though, I placed unreasonable expectations on the quality and nature of the response in relation to my initial message. For example, if I sent a page-long, detailed email to a friend and got only two sentences back, my immediate assumption was that the recipient either did not care or did not even read everything that I had taken the time and effort to write. I personally put a lot of careful thought into how I phrase things, intentionally selecting words and punctuation so as to avoid being misunderstood or giving off the wrong "tone." (I have gotten a lot of flak for that, by the way – the impossibility of identifying one's tone in written messages – but I still hold to the belief that you can!) So when that friend does not put forth an equal effort, according to me, I interpreted that as indifference. Never mind how offended I would get if I received no response at all!

I finally accepted the fact that I was reading into stuff way too much, and it almost always ended up doing more harm than good. I also really needed to get a life! I say that because once I started getting busier at work and home and more preoccupied with my own children, my own responses to others became shorter. They were still prompt and well-thought-out, but very much abridged.

That said, I continue to find a lack of response to be problematic when hosting certain family members for a nice meal. We do not often have the opportunity to prepare home-cooked meals for my in-laws, but when we do, my husband and I both put a lot of hard work into them. My father-in-law usually thanks us afterwards, but he tends to be the only one who does so, which leaves me wondering later if no one else appreciated the effort, let alone enjoyed the food. I do not necessarily expect compliments, but a simple thank you after a meal is fairly normal, even amongst family. I find the absence of any such gratitude or feedback to be uncomfortable and rather insulting, but I suppose my different culture and upbringing should be kept in consideration here. In any case, I try to not dwell on or become bitter about it.

Towards the end of 2011, I became fascinated by a particular actor who was still an up-and-coming celebrity at the time. Primarily in an effort to connect with him, I joined Twitter. He had about 10,000 followers back then, and often responded to fans' tweets. I occasionally tweeted him, along with a few other actors I like, always hoping for a response, but never fully expecting one. I also sent him a letter with a postage-paid return envelope and a photo of him to autograph. None of that was outlandish, and on the surface I looked like any normal fan; but it did not take long to recognize the true motivation underneath it all: to feel validated. And not just any validation, but that from someone famous.

To date he has not responded, but I did get a response on two separate occasions from another actor, and both times I experienced a brief euphoric high that further proved the point. The frustrating part about that type of validation is that it is temporary, superficial, and impersonal. Inspiring and exciting, maybe, but fleeting and ultimately pointless. The euphoria manifested as an adrenaline rush, followed very quickly by a bum-out once reality pulled me out of the clouds. But...I recognized the futility of seeking that type of validation, and even though I wished I had been as lucky as those fans who did receive responses, my happiness and worth did not depend upon it. Those people don't know me and have zero obligation to me, so it is absolutely nothing personal. If I were famous, would I reply to my fans' tweets? I think I would try to, but everyone has their own style and preferences; plus, they are busy and surely cannot be expected to read, let alone acknowledge, hundreds to thousands of messages per day!

I sometimes find myself chasing my own false hopes until it becomes an unhealthy obsession. Through therapy, I learned that the perpetuating of my obsessions is my dysfunctional coping mechanism. When something legitimately "bad" happens in my life, I automatically fixate upon certain things or people. It is what I know. Whenever something bad happened to my mom, she did the same thing, except her OCD coping mechanism manifested strongly as hoarding. This pattern became evident in my own life when simultaneously had to deal with the death of Billy's grandmother and a friend's suicide, followed immediately by my having to move from a large office with windows at work to a small office with no windows (on a cold, miserable winter day). I held it together on the outside, but my emotional health took a dive, and I found myself once again focusing on my go-to obsessions.

My objective now is to catch myself in the act of obsessing, and redirect my focus on to the negative event or circumstance in my life in order to deal with the real issue at hand in a healthy, productive, acceptable way.

Shortly after becoming aware of the coping thing, I caught myself starting to obsess hard over the aforementioned actor, and I started to replay over and over in my head the night that I sort of met him on the red carpet at a movie premiere (I was merely a spectator on the opposite side of the velvet rope). I was beating myself up for not being more aggressive with trying to get a photo with him that night. I was even harder on myself for not attending a previous movie premiere that had a much smaller turnout, where fans were much more successful in meeting him. I would further torment myself by reading an article on him and his recent work, or watching interviews with him online, or re-reading his Twitter feed. The whole thing was making me sick to my stomach, literally. Suddenly I was reminded that a very close friend had just ended our friendship, which had devastated me and shattered my spirit. The light bulb went on and I said out loud to myself, "I am dysfunctionally coping. Stop obsessing." It didn't make everything go away or get better on the spot, but it was effective in snapping me out of the distraction – which is all this was.

But I'm getting ahead of myself now. What follows here are recaps of some particular sessions that provided me with tremendous insight.

> 3/20/12 - Today my therapist advised that when I find myself losing control, recognize that the feeling is *activated* by the circumstance, but is not necessarily directly part of it. Take a step back and don't project old patterns onto the current situation. When I expect someone to fulfill a request to do something, but it does not get done (at all, let alone *my* way) or even acknowledged, there is a direct parallel to the disregard I felt when Mom would not clean the house despite years of pleading. I recently found my-

self angry with someone for not calling me, per my requests, and I felt like I was going crazy because it seemed as though I was not getting through to her. I thought she was either ignoring me or misunderstanding me. I could not influence the desired result with her, and therefore, I was not in control. Interestingly, this person was an older woman. When I mentioned this to my psychologist, she immediately made the connection to my childhood and the damaged lines of communication between my mother and me, as well as my own impotence over her. A part of my subconscious switched on again, and said, "Here we go again. More disregard by a woman who is older than you." *Stop. Recognize. Take a step back.*

I believe I eventually I turned into a control freak because I had none growing up. Often when a situation manifests itself as one in which I have zero control, my immediate response is to go on the defensive. I cannot count the various times and ways I have demonstrated passive-aggressive behavior in the past, but I am trying my darndest to avoid that moving forward.

4/3 – I acknowledged my tendency to automatically blame myself for any negative response I get from a friend. Twice in the past month, with two different people, things seemed "off" during my attempts to connect and communicate, and my immediate response was, *What did I do now?* I knew with certainty that I had done nothing, but figured maybe something I said was taken the wrong way...or maybe they heard some rumor about me from someone else? Whatever it was, I seem to take the lack of explanation way too personally, assuming the worst, and then I become resentful of the person for not telling me what's wrong. There are a million and one possibilities why someone doesn't respond to a text or email, or answer their phone, or why someone is brief and unemotional if or when he/she does respond. ONE of those possibilities MIGHT have something to do with me, but if my conscience is clear, chances are, I'm not the reason. For too long, however, my initial thought has always been, "It's my fault." Whenever this happens, I literally get an upset stomach and feel extremely uneasy until I am convinced their tone/attitude/shortness/avoidance is not in any way linked to me. Of course, by then, I have annoyed the person by asking more than once if they're "SURE everything's OK," etc. and then feel sheepish when I come to find out their dog just died, or their dad was just diagnosed with cancer, or they are dealing with something legitimately upsetting. The frustrating reality is that it is almost *never* linked to me, yet I waste so much energy worrying that it is. The worst-case scenarios that haunt me are purely imagined.

Apparently the dazed world in which I've been living disregards the fact that most mature people confront their friends if they have offended them...so if I haven't been confronted, and even more, have already been told once that I've done nothing wrong, I must, MUST accept that at face value and not question it. I'm so good at saying, "I can't be held accountable for something I'm not aware of," but have struggled with believing it my entire life. Even when I know my conscience is clear, I get lost in the nagging "What If's" that inevitably spiral out of control into a dark place where friendships ultimately go to die.

Looking back it is highly probable that I subconsciously felt blamed for the emotional nurture I lacked as a child. Today when my therapist asked me why that would have been the case, I jokingly replied, "Maybe my mom secretly resented my existence because I was just taking up space in her house...where boxes and stuff could have been." My therapist responded to my mockery with seriousness and said I was on to something. Digging deeper on this, it became clear that the absence of my own space coupled with the absence of my mother – sometimes physically, sometimes emotionally – led to quiet, buried feelings of worthlessness. My mom used to repeatedly joke about selling me or trading me in during department store "baby sales." If I got offended, that offended her, as if my own feelings did not matter. Nevertheless I felt unwanted. I was born late in my parents' life, and often heard that they had almost given up on getting pregnant. I was a happy miracle; but maybe in her heart, my mom had already moved on and resigned herself to the idea of never having a child, so by the time I came along, they were comfortable in their little life. I changed everything for them. Maybe she regretted having me?

Or maybe not. But if somehow my subconscious picked up on any of this while I was growing up, it is no wonder I am so quick to blame myself for things.

So, all these years of self-doubt and paranoia, which not only made me anxious but also caused me to eventually offend and push away some of my most precious friends, are linked yet again to the representation of the crap in my parents' house? How INSANELY frustrating. But…blame does not cancel out blame, and it is what it is. *So recognize it, and move on.*

It is important to note that I always knew my parents loved me, and my physical needs were always met. There was no abuse or neglect. There was just always something missing. I never knew what it was. Even though I was a "good kid," I often acted out for attention as a young child. At the same time, I was a bit of an overachiever, which was just the manifestation of my soul crying out for approval and positive attention. I was overcompensating with good grades and scholastic accolades that reassured me of my "value." Similarly, it is possible that my parents tried to overcompensate for the lack of emotional nurture by taking us on nice family vacations, dining at fine restaurants, sending me to good schools, and being lenient with how I spent my free time and who I hung around. Not that I did not appreciate all of that, but it was still just a substitute for what I truly needed.

5/1 – We started talking about the way Mom made me feel when I was growing up. What comes to the surface most automatically and prominently are resentment and frustration. Her attempts at showing affection toward me, as well as any vulnerability in general (i.e. her crying when someone died) made me supremely uncomfortable. The emotion I most often remember her exhibiting is anger or frustration. She was constantly restless. She also made herself the victim and/or center of attention a lot.

I reminisced about the baby shower she threw for me back home, which was nearly a disaster. I do not consider myself a prima donna by any means, but it was MY DAY...something you get to celebrate only once. Her only child was bringing her first grandchild into the world! It became completely about her, embarrassing me and making everyone else uncomfortable in the process.

We were home visiting for about a week, and I was so excited to see my friends and family. During one of our days at the beach, my hubby and I were struck with the most severe sunburn either of us had ever experienced in our lives. My burn was the worst on my legs and feet, such that I could barely walk, but I was determined to not let that ruin the remainder of our visit.

A day before the party, my dad called me. He was calm, but I could hear concern in his voice. "Mel, I don't want you to worry, but Mom is in the hospital." He said they were out buying decorations for the party and she suddenly became nonresponsive to him, so his first reaction was to take her to the ER. He assured me that she was OK, but said she possibly overdosed on her cocktail of medicine she takes for pain, anxiety, etc. (my mom later swore to us that that was not the case. I still don't know what the heck happened.), but the party was still on. Anyway, the next day, as we were getting ready to leave for the party, we got a call to wait because things weren't ready yet. First 15 minutes, then 30, then I started feeling anxious about the guests. Were they just THERE, sitting as my mom rushed around frantically tying things together and doing God-knows-what that could not have been done an hour ago? After 45 minutes or so, we finally decided to head over.

I arrived to my baby shower and was greeted by my mother exclaiming, "You're not supposed to be here yet! We're not ready!" with unreserved exasperation. I reminded her that the party was to start at whatever-time, and then asked how she was doing, to which she muttered she did not want to talk about it. Of course she did not even *notice* that I could barely walk due to the sunburn. To make matters worse, you could tell the guests felt awkward about being there, especially those who saw her "greeting" upon our arrival. Some offered to help her, which only seemed to frustrate her more. Shortly after we showed up, one couple had to take off. They did not even get to eat! By then I was furious, but didn't want to make anyone feel more uncomfortable, so I bit my tongue and kept going around greeting and hugging everyone. Many people – immediate family, mostly – did not even show up, and I could not help but wonder if they were just avoiding my mom. This erratic, off-putting behavior was typical of her when she was under stress.

Once the food was available and she calmed down, we all started enjoying ourselves. She got worked up again at the end, though, when it was time to clean up. I guess she felt like she didn't have enough help, even though people offered again, but she gave the impression that she expected ME to pitch in. Normally I would, but this was my freaking BABY SHOWER, and did I mention I could barely walk? I finally brought that to her attention. My friends and I wanted to try and hang out afterwards, so they had to sneak away, too, lest they be laden with guilt.

I felt completely unwelcome and undervalued by my own mother at what was otherwise supposed to be a tremendous moment of celebration and happy excitement. Contrast that with the baby shower my in-laws threw for me, where I did feel celebrated and the overall tone was so much more relaxed and jubilant. It wasn't perfect, but it was for me. About me. And I did not feel guilty leaving without cleaning up!

I know Mom tries. She means well. It just never seemed that she was capable of expressing love toward me in the way I needed it most. She always gave me lots of little gifts, but I did not get the emotional nurturing I truly needed and rightly deserved from her. It would later become evident to me that words of affirmation (or verbal affirmation) was my primary "love language," but more on that later. So one of two things may have occurred: a) Gifts were never my love language to begin with, so I did not translate them into "love," and therefore felt lacking; or b) Because I felt lacking already, I rejected that love language on purpose.

> 5/15 – We talked about Mother's Day. Billy and I had sent a package to my parents and my Dad acknowledged receipt, but Mom said nothing. On Sunday, we called, but she didn't answer (no surprise); so my toddler and I left her a message. No call back. The next day, I called Mom again to see if she liked the stuff I sent. She said yeah, and the message "from Rory"

was cute (forget me). She never wished me a happy Mother's Day back, never asked me how I was doing (as usual). She spent the latter half of our conversation talking about a young adult boy from their church who she "connects with" and to whom her heart goes out because he takes medication like she does, or something. I sat there listening, stunned, confused, amused, disregarded. I found it interesting that she feels the need to nurture *others*, including my elderly father (Billy observed that she sometimes treats him like a child), considering the lack of nurture bestowed upon me. Perhaps it is her motherly instinct kicking in, which she erroneously feels I am no longer in need of?

I also shared how my relationship with my mother-in-law feels superficial and sometimes strained or forced, but my therapist was quick to point out that she is not to blame for how I feel. I am projecting my damaged relationship with my own mother on to my relationship with her. No matter how hard my mother-in-law (or anyone else) tries to express care/concern for me, it will never be sufficient. I will always hunger for *my* mother's love, and cannot rely on others to change in order to cater to me or fill that void. When I get angry, the way to overcome my anger is to question every circumstance that upsets me. Ask: Did the person wrong me or do something wrong, or am I projecting?

Additionally, we reviewed the "homework" assignment from the previous session, which is as follows.

How do these words NOT apply to my relationship with my mother, as an adult as well as when I was a child?

CELEBRATED
Once in a while, after some great achievement, she would tell me she was proud of me. She always took pictures at ceremonies…usually awkward, candid ones, and often dark or blurry. Sometimes she wrote poems for or about me, or she rewarded me with gifts, but I never FELT genuine praise or appreciation from her. I never heard her brag about me to people. These days people will tell me, "Your mom talks

about you all the time! She's so proud of you!" but she *rarely* expresses any of these good thoughts/feelings toward me directly. She will say things like, "Your dad really misses you," but she never says it about herself. She managed to ruin the baby shower she threw for me, and was a major downer on events leading up to my wedding. Our wedding gift to both of our parents was an engraved silver picture frame with one of our wedding photos. I have no idea where theirs is.

TAKEN CARE OF / VALUED
Her stuff always seemed more important than me. There were times I almost felt neglected by her while I was growing up because she was often absent, and whenever she was around, she was tired or grumpy. Early on she did prep food/meals at times, but Dad raised me for the most part. Our "family time" was our traveling together, attending events, or going out to eat, but she never asked me how I was doing, and rarely gave feedback when I'd bring it up on my own. She never seemed interested in me. Now, she never calls, and when I call, she does most of the talking and never asks how any of us are doing. I have to proactively tell her – even after I've already called her out on that. She generally seems to not care.

RELAXED / HAPPY / POSITIVE
Sadly, I have never known her to be a serene or peaceful spirit. She herself says she cannot relax, and if she does sit still for a while, she falls asleep. Her constant fidgeting and anxiety have always made me uncomfortable and nervous or anxious. She often embarrassed me with her appearance, her carrying excessive bags wherever she goes, and the way she asks for things in public (i.e. ordering food in a restaurant). Also, her moods varied unpredictably, and she has a short temper. The primary emotion/demeanor I associate with her is irritation, which she exhibits even when someone is trying to help her.

GRATEFUL
It has always been difficult for me to say "thank you" to her, even in the best of times. I have always figured her nice gestures were either obligatory or just overcompensation for her absence and the unlivable condition of the house. It's hard to be grateful to someone who robbed you of a normal childhood and didn't even give you your "own" room growing up, no matter what else they do to try and make up for it later. She often gave/gives little gifts to me, but it's usually nothing I want/need. If I tell her I like something, she fixates on that and buys it for me until I get tired of it. Her pride makes it difficult to correct her or clarify something questionable; for that reason, she made my bridesmaids bouquets completely wrong. They were nothing close to what I wanted, but rather than show me her ideas, she went ahead and made them, and was offended when I told her the morning of my wedding that they weren't what I'd had in mind (she asked).

When I got home from my session, my Mother's Day card had arrived in the mail from my parents. My mom wrote a poem, which was nice, but seems to be the only way she ever expresses any sentiment towards me. I still found it unsatisfyingly odd that she had nothing to say to me on the phone the day before.

6/7 – I had called a woman older than me to apologize if I have ever come across as anything less than respectful. We had some previous misunderstandings and I just wanted to clear the air. She said she appreciated that, but she had moved past it all and everything was fine. That night I resolved out loud to stop being paranoid that my friends were upset with me. If my conscience was clear of offending someone, I would no longer assume otherwise. If a friend looks at me "wrong," doesn't say hi to me, doesn't reply to a text or answer my phone call, etc., I'm not going to blame myself anymore. Unless confronted, I have done nothing wrong. I'm so sick and tired of worrying about that, especially since I am overly conscious of being polite (to everyone in general) and showing my friends I care about them.

6/12 – We discussed my need to take a short break from church…not my FAITH, just the perceived drama connected to some people and the hurt it has recently caused. My fear with that, with any distance with anyone, is my lifelong issue of tension that I tend to imagine – thinking someone doesn't like me anymore, or has replaced me, or isn't interested in me now, etc. This happens far too often, and has occurred for as long as I can remember. My therapist suggested being the proactive one when I do go back – i.e. walking up to people I haven't seen for a while and initiating a catch-up chat. She said to "be amazing" and make THEM feel special; give THEM attention and be interested in THEM, regardless of how much I'll feel like crap if they don't seem to care about ME at all. What really resonated was her reminder that other people generally want to feel cared about just as much as I do. Somebody has to make the first move, and it cannot ALWAYS be them. I cannot just sit back and expect people to flock to me.

8/7 – We are tackling anger issues now. I admitted that whenever I get angry at someone, I never deal with it properly. I tend to vent to others about someone offending me ("triangulate" – because a third person gets indirectly involved), rather than confronting the offender directly. When I do muster up the guts to confront someone, a friend or otherwise, I almost always come across wrong. When asked why I think I do this (not deal with the offender directly), I again referred to interactions with my mom. No matter how calmly I tried to address an issue with her, I was met with anything but receptiveness. I would walk away defeated, feeling bad for opening my mouth, and sometimes feeling MORE angry with her. Instead of learning to deal with negative feelings, I learned to walk on eggshells. And I started to do it with everyone, even friends. The only people I have ever been "raw" with were Billy, past boyfriends, and (most unfortunately) my daughter. But then, it comes out explosively, because all the pent-up frustration, offenses, and hurts – from them as well as others – would come to a head and get let out. I know it's not fair to them, and it's certainly not healthy for me. And I REALLY don't want my daughter to think it's OK to act like that, especially as an adult. I told my therapist I want to start working on this by focusing on taking stuff less personally, especially with close friends and family (specifically, my in-laws).

My therapist noted that anger is an easier emotion to access than sadness because it is less vulnerable, and I need to get to the point where I can cry about my mom and our situation. Maybe someday...but not today.

In weeks following, I gently confronted my father-in-law, mother-in-law, and sister-in-law about various issues that had been bothering me. I do not feel that much was resolved for the long-term, but it was helpful to get stuff off my chest.

9/18 – We uncovered the fact that Mom's hoarding is the result of a deep pain that she may or may not even realize she has. In the midst of the clean-up, as I noted in my "Hoarders" journal, she broke down and stated that her parents did not love her, etc. Maybe they didn't. Or maybe they did, but they did not express their love in a way that she would recognize or appreciate. Subsequently, she has loved me, but her expressions of love have been in the only ways she knew and not in the way I needed. I mentioned that my primary love language is words of affirmation. Is that any surprise for someone who is constantly seeking validation? What came first, though? Was it that I was wired to feel love when I was affirmed, or did I crave the affirmation because I lacked it all this time? Maybe both? In any case, I never fully felt loved as a teen or young adult. The love was always there, but it did not fulfill me. So I sought love, affection, attention, etc. from others, namely guys and older women. My highest goal now as a mother is to break that cycle and ensure my own children actually FEEL the unconditional love one fundamentally needs from his or her own mother, and then teach them how to love.

To elaborate on the "love language" topic that I have repeatedly alluded to, here is an excerpt from another one of my blog posts, from August 2011:

> We need to be conscientiously sensitive to our loved ones when they are the ones suffering. Pay attention and respond, and at least make an effort to meet their emotional needs. One of my dad's friends recently passed away from melanoma. He could easily have fought it and won, but he purposely didn't bother. My dad asked him why he didn't seek treatment, or even go back to the doctor after he was diagnosed. He replied, "I don't really fit in here. It doesn't matter either way." My dad and their other friends allegedly had NO idea that he felt this way. He either hid his depression very well, or they weren't paying attention – or perhaps both. That saddened me, and was yet another slap in my face to remind me to LOVE the people I care about in a way that THEY will recognize it.
>
> Several years ago, Christian author Gary Chapman wrote a book entitled *The Five Love Languages*. Though it sparked some debate

within the Christian community, I liked it and personally identified with it.

Since reading the book about 10 years ago, it has become apparent to me that my "love languages" are words of affirmation, followed by acts of service. That's what makes me tick. When people express their care for me in those ways, I feel "loved." That doesn't mean I don't appreciate gifts, hugs (personal touch), or quality time, but without positive words, and the actions that speak louder than those words, I don't quite feel fulfilled. You can argue against that philosophy all you want, or call it by whatever name you wish, but that is the way I am wired. Whether you subscribe to this thinking or not, we ALL have different things that make us feel loved and validated. Dr. Chapman tries to simplify all those different things into 5 general categories, which may or may not be "all-inclusive"; but I believe the point he tries to get across is universal.

I recently came to the discouraging realization that most of the people in my life don't speak my "love language" to me. Now, I can wallow in self-pity or alienate myself because "no one cares about me, so screw them all"; OR I can communicate my needs/desires to those closest to me, and be graceful towards them when they don't know how to express their love, or when they forget. Let's face it, I suck at gift-giving, but I know some people who feel most loved when they receive a gift. I make it a point to step outside of MY comfort zone and buy them a gift, because I want them to know that that's how much they mean to me. If I spoke MY love language to them, showering them with praise and encouragement, that would be nice...but probably not enough. Something would feel lacking. Loving someone the way YOU want to be loved is like saying, "I love you" to them in a language foreign to him. You're saying exactly what he wants to hear, and you mean well; the problem is, he does not understand you. Speak his language.

My point in bringing all that up is simply this: Make sure your loved ones REALLY KNOW that you love them. Make sure they REALLY KNOW that they matter. Even if you're the only one in the whole world who shows them they're cared about or thought of, BE THAT PERSON. It could make a day. It could save a life.

I love this song, co-written by Garth Brooks and popularized in the late '90s by Joose: "If tomorrow never comes, will she know how much I loved her? Did I try in every way to show her every day that she's my only one? [...] 'Cause I've lost loved ones in my life who never knew how much I loved them. Now I live with the regret that my true feelings for them never were revealed. So I made a promise to myself to say each day how much she means to me, and avoid that circumstance where there's no second chance to tell her how I feel..." If you take the song out of its romantic context, it applies to everyone we deeply care about.

This topic would come up again and again at home, and continues to affect my relationships with those closest to me when I let it. I still struggle with speaking up about it because honestly, it feels pathetic and self-seeking to ask for people to love me MY way, but I will keep working on it. Beyond that, I am trying to accept that everyone loves in his or her own way, and appreciate others' efforts to express themselves at all, even if it is not quite what I want or need.

10/2 – Just as an alcoholic can't just have one drink to escape, I can't use fantasy to escape. It messes me up. I get high off it, but then I crash. I actually have to be careful watching movies, plays, etc. I am prone to fixating on a character, actor, story line, or concept – especially when I'm going through something bad (remember, obsessing is my dysfunctional coping mechanism). Fantasy is "safe" because it's not real; it can't hurt me. So I escape. But when I snap back to reality, I get so quickly and easily bummed out, knowing that fantasy can't (or most likely won't) ever happen.

So, I had to ask, what's up with my fascination with capes and masks? I wouldn't call it a fetish, but there's something "sexy" about them. Billy says I'm using the wrong word, but I don't know how else to describe it. They disturb me in a good way? Anyway, one Halloween when I was about 8 or 9 years old, a group of trick-or-treaters stopped in my driveway where we gave out candy, as I was getting ready to go around the neighborhood with my dad. All of their faces were masked or covered, so I didn't know who they were, but one of them said cheerfully, "Hi, Melissa!" I think s/he was a vampire or zombie or something. I waved and said, "Hi" back, but never found out who it was. Something about that encounter gave me butterflies. I acknowledged the escape from reality, but wondered why I would find it sexy. We never really got to the bottom of this, but my therapist suggested there was something about the mystery, or the role-play, that was appealing to me – again, it is fantasy.

11/27 – We talked about feeling accepted and fitting in. Growing up I never really felt like I "fit in." I was casually acquainted with everyone and friendly with many, but I usually had one best friend and always stuck with her, feeling awkward and lonely when she wasn't there. I now find myself in situations where I'm the youngest (i.e. church Bible studies or women's retreats), and find it odd and somewhat discouraging that even then I feel out of place or borderline unwelcome. Where's the nurture, the mentorship? It's not that I feel excluded, there's just no effort to include me. I guess what I really desire is to be taken under someone's wing. In most social groups, I start out on the shy side and I am not the type to butt into a conversation or try to include myself. Either I feel rude, clueless, or completely disinterested at the topic being discussed.

Now I worry less about myself and more about my daughter. It breaks my heart whenever I catch her at school by herself or being ignored by her friends. My therapist warned me of becoming enmeshed or overprotective, lest she not learn to take care of herself and establish her own voice and identity. I must be careful to not project onto her my own insecurities and beware of cognitive dissonance; that is, turning something benign into something negative. She is a happy kid, so I have no real reason to be concerned right now, but I am always keeping an eye on her social skills and interactions.

1/22/13 – The last couple months I have been recovering from a special friendship that ended unexpectedly, so a large portion of our recent sessions has revolved around that. Today we talked about parenting, and why I lose my temper with my toddler so quickly…and how *badly* I want to change that. I have started observing her yelling at and sternly scolding her dolls and stuffed animals when she's playing, which was a slap in my face. She is learning this from her parents! From ME! My therapist recommended three books on the topic of raising a happy child, and challenged me to locate the "triggers" that are setting me off.

We also discussed my loathing of being late anywhere, and how I get so irritable when my daughter slows me down in the morning. I rush through our precious short time together in the morning, and then feel guilty afterwards because I did not appreciate that time at all, and was more focused on getting to work 5 minutes earlier than I did. I get riled up and frustrated, which my therapist identified as anxiety – a trait I am certain I inherited from my mother. She went on to connect the anxiety to my lack of control in the situation. I can control when I get out of bed and how long it takes *me* to get ready in the morning, and I know when to leave the house to make it to work by a certain time; but throwing a toddler into the mix presents an element of unpredictability that could alter my routine, thus removing it from my control. I have been trying to become more conscious of when I start to rush, especially in the mornings, so that I maintain my composure and positivity at the very least, but more so to *enjoy* my time with my little girl.

I went into today's session (and several previous ones) with no agenda and no list of problems, intending to reduce the frequency of our appointments from bi-weekly to monthly; but every time I walk out, it is clear to me that I still have a long way to go!

2/19 – I finished reading *Raising Happiness: 10 Simple Steps for More Joyful Kids and Happier Parents* (Christine Carter), one of the books my therapist recommended, and shared the things I liked and learned. We spent most of the session, however, discussing my relationship with my in-laws, which is relatively positive compared to many others' out there, but still lacking in many ways. My complaints range from the petty and almost silly – for example, it frustrates me that, after nine years, they still call me Melissa, instead of Mel, which they know I prefer to be known by amongst family and friends – to more serious issues, such as how lenient they are with my daughter when she is in their care (i.e. allowing lots of visual stimulation and sugar and regularly foregoing naps). I am also constantly being picked on about my body weight. Even though my weight is normal for my height and frame, my mother-in-law has made innumerable comments about how small I am and the need to fatten me up, which I fail to find the humor in and certainly do not take as a compliment. Despite voicing my dislike for these ridiculous comments, they don't stop, and it's beyond annoying.

I have taken offense to certain things that others might just laugh off. Some things have been addressed with them, but in general, I feel disrespected and disregarded. My therapist challenged me to speak up when appropriate, but otherwise accept our differences and not take everything personally (a life-long struggle of mine!). I can acknowledge to myself that it makes me sad to not have the relationship I really want, but – once again – I *must* be careful to not project onto my in-laws what I expect but did not get from my own parents.

3/19 – I am still losing my temper with my three-year-old, which always makes me feel so sad and guilty after it happens. I do not feel like I'm getting better with it, BUT I am much more conscious of when it's about to happen, or at least while it is happening. My anger is not mindless, I realize it's a problem, and I'm determined to change. My therapist encouraged me to think outside the box when dealing with certain power struggles (i.e. the fight to get her to brush her teeth…EVERY DAY), and walk out of the room if I need a "time out" from the situation.

We also talked about someone within my company who has been a tremendous source of stress and frustration to my coworkers and me on a regular basis. We agreed that I have been allowing her to stress me out much more than necessary, though, by getting involved in conversations about her and listening to others' complaints about her. My therapist noted that I get drawn into the drama; but while others have the ability to talk about her and move on, I get a charge because hearing everyone else share the same negative opinion about her *validates* my own feelings. She said I should acknowledge my own feelings, but it is probably best to keep them to myself. This is going to be tough, especially since I value the validation so strongly, but I agreed that it is necessary for my mental health.

4/2 – I have been feeling anxious and pessimistic about my current (second) pregnancy. Whereas my first pregnancy was "text book" – predictable and smooth – this one has had some unpleasant surprises (including sharp abdominal pains, multiple contaminated urine samples, spontaneous nosebleeds, and not being able to get an immediate read on the baby's heartbeat at 14 weeks). Since everything went so well last time, my expectations are high...but not being met. So now I'm in between stages, where the nausea has subsided but I am not yet showing nor feeling the baby move, and I worry about the baby between each check-up. I worry that God knows there is a small part of me that is not 100% on board with having another baby, for entirely selfish reasons, and that God will take it away from me if I feel or think anything but joy and excitement. I know that's an unfair, ludicrous imagination that is not even consistent with the nature of God, but it makes me nervous nonetheless. My therapist said I have to accept the fact that I'm feeling ambivalent right now, and know that that's OK. Moreover, if (God forbid) something should happen to this baby, it is NOT my fault or because of any of those ambivalent thoughts I may have had. She said to honor my feelings and don't think there is anything wrong with me for having them. That was encouraging, and can be applied to many apprehensions and doubts beyond this pregnancy.

I often wonder what my therapist really thinks of me – like when I walk out, does she think, "Oy, that one…" Overall I think I have done a good job of keeping her mentally categorized as my therapist, and not as my friend. Nothing she says offends me, even when she is totally blunt, and that is precisely the relationship I need! It is a liberating feeling, really…to *not care*. To feel safe enough to hold nothing back and be totally raw. To have someone to listen to my problems, and not feel the need to apologize for taking up their time or burdening them with some secret information. I am going to miss her when our sessions are over.

> 4/30 – We focused primarily on my relationships with my daughter and my mother-in-law again. The key challenge and take-away for both was to not personalize everything negative. My daughter's misbehavior is not always a poor reflection on me or my parenting skills. Most of the time, she's just being a three-year-old. I shouldn't feel guilty or like a failure every day, even though I often do – especially when I raise my voice. Talking to other parents of toddlers (friends at church, coworkers, parents of her classmates and at gymnastics, etc.) has been encouraging because it helps me realize she is totally normal for her age! Even the most "together" parents have shared tales of woe similar to my own.
>
> Nothing particularly upsetting has happened recently with my in-laws, but a benign Facebook comment my mother-in-law left on my page triggered the ongoing discontent I have about our relationship; it was a reminder that she does not demonstrate care for me in the way that I *need*. Too often it seems all of my in-laws do not know how to relate to me, never asking me how I am doing – it's always, "How are your parents?" or now that I am pregnant, "How's the baby?" I do not need them to constantly ask me how I feel, etc., but when they ask the peripheral questions or find a way to laugh off – or completely disregard – something serious, it is a painful reminder that I lack the care I yearn for and desire from my own family. When it comes down to it, they all really know so very little about me.

I was baffled about my inability to address this with my mother-in-law in particular, and my therapist helped me realize it is likely because I never got what I needed relationally from my own mother whenever I voiced my discontent. So why put myself out on a limb, just to be blown off? The reality is that I am not going to get what I want until I ask for it, and she may be completely clueless that there is anything missing from our relationship. She, and everyone else, may not think there's anything wrong, so it really is entirely on me to fix that. I was *again* reminded to not project my relationship with my mother on to my mother-in-law, and keep my expectations reasonable.

In May we reduced our appointment frequency to monthly (or every 4 weeks). This was partly due to insurance co-pays going up, but honestly, I feel like we are running out of things to talk about. That is a good thing, I think! At this point, I have started demonstrating a repeat of patterns in my behavior and thought processes that tell us nothing new besides the fact that the pattern exists. I know I still have a long way to go, but I have learned much and am now trying to apply it all to how I think and react.

7/23 – At the end of our previous session (June), I expressed my biggest concern regarding my parents' visit in Sept-Oct, when they come out for the baby's birth – namely, my mother's hoarding tendencies coming with her into our home, as it did the last time they visited. We talked about this in depth during this session, and my therapist stressed the fact that I should not expect my mom to change her behavior while she's here. Like asking a serious alcoholic to not drink for a month while he's staying in my house, just because it's my house, and expecting him to comply, I can't ask my mom to cease all hoarding tendencies. By inviting her into our home, we are accepting her as she is. I have to work on accepting my mom for who she is, flaws and all, just like I would anyone else in my life I care about. I'm far from perfect and would hope to be accepted as I am by my friends and family, too.

We talked about how I had asked my mom to find and bring my old Barbie dolls for my daughter, and how excited I am at the prospect of giving them to her, but realistically I need to prepare for disappointment because she probably won't be able to dig them out in time. I have spent my life being disappointed when it came to matters having anything to do with my parents' house – even the smallest, easiest requests – and I'm tired of it. My therapist asked me how I can protect myself from feeling that constant disappointment. I thought for a minute and said, "Stop asking." As unfair as I feel that is to me, I can't change her…but I *can* change my outlook on the situation. I often have high expectations of others because I am so self-conscious of the way I act (or speak, etc.). I have to "lower" my expectations for my mom – again, so that I can more easily accept her. It's not the same as condoning her behavior, and she knows that. But then I asked how I prevent that from spilling into all my other relationships. I still have high expectations for everyone else; do I need to lower them across the board? Probably. I tend to be unreasonable at times with pretty much everyone.

Later on a different topic, I said of someone else, "I want to hate her, but at the same time, I want to be loved and appreciated by her. I want her to miss me when I'm gone." My therapist said this was very telling and reflects the identical sentiments I seem to feel toward my mother. In both situations, as well as in the case with my mother-in-law, that "lacking" feeling can be narrowed down to the absence of verbal affirmation, which I so desperately and regularly crave and do not receive from the ones I expect it from. In the themes throughout my life, the most strained relationships fall into that category, but I know if I do not specifically ask for that which I am missing, I may never get it. (See the patterns yet? Like I said, nothing new.) I'm not quite there yet, though – asking for the affirmation, that is.

With another baby on the way in October, my parents coming into town, and my husband's schedule anticipated to become extremely hectic next year, I decided to end my therapy sessions for the time being. I met with my therapist once more on 8/20/13. I reiterated with the utmost gratitude how much I have learned. I had low expectations going into therapy but came out a very different person. It is so important to understand that it is never the job of a mental health professional to "fix" you, and that the sole responsibility to change lies with you. I am thankful to have people in my life that encouraged me to seek the help I so desperately needed and I am honestly terrified to imagine what I would be without it!

Chapter 5: Science

Hoarding is often misunderstood amongst those who have no first-hand exposure to it. Most of the hoarders I have crossed paths with in my life prefer to refer to themselves as "pack-rats" or "collectors" because "hoarder" is simply too harsh. It is associated with such a negative stigma and even makes them sound like they carry a contagious disease or something. In fact, compulsive hoarding is a mental disorder that requires professional treatment to appropriately address and overcome it.

Hoarders.org tells us that in 1996, subject matter experts Randy O. Frost, Ph.D. and Tamara L. Hartl, Ph.D. "provided the first systematic definition, identifying three characteristics: '(1) the acquisition of, and failure to discard a large number of possessions that appear to be useless or of limited value; (2) living spaces sufficiently cluttered so as to preclude activities for which those spaces were designed; and (3) significant distress or impairment in functioning caused by the hoarding.' This definition distinguished hoarding from the collecting of objects generally considered interesting and valuable."

The Mayo Clinic defines hoarding as follows: "Hoarding is the excessive collection of items, along with the inability to discard them. Hoarding often creates such cramped living conditions that homes may be filled to capacity, with only narrow pathways winding through stacks of clutter. Some people also collect animals, keeping dozens or hundreds of pets often in unsanitary conditions. Hoarding, also called compulsive hoarding and compulsive hoarding syndrome, may be a symptom of obsessive-compulsive disorder (OCD). But many people who hoard don't have other OCD-related symptoms. People who hoard often don't see it as a problem, making treatment challenging. But intensive treatment can help people who hoard understand their compulsions and live safer, more enjoyable lives."

The key here is the *inability to discard* items, as the Mayo Clinic website notes above. This is the heart of why hoarding is a disorder and – like many other mental health issues that are not easily explained – the reason why it is both extremely frustrating and difficult to grasp for those who are not personally dealing with it. Having lived through it, and subsequently receiving counseling as a result, I have a much better grasp of it, but logically I still struggle with WHY she cannot just let go of certain things. I cannot get inside her head enough to pinpoint exactly when this started, or if this was something to which she was already predisposed, but she has shared "clues" along the way that suggest it was triggered by loss and invalidation. Even more vexing for me is that I can do little else beyond accepting that this is something my mom struggles with until she chooses to make a change.

During my "Hoarders" pre-taping interview with Dr. Chabaud, she recommended that I visit the Children of Hoarders website (childrenofhoarders.com). She said it would help me better understand this disorder, and in turn, my mother – but it would also be of great value to me personally. I made note of it, but didn't actually take the time to look at any content until I started therapy and decided I wanted to learn more about the cause and effect between hoarders and the issues their children develop. Once I started reading and exploring the site, I could not stop. While the stories were circumstantially unique, the consequences and struggles now faced by the other children of hoarders echoed my very own – in some cases, identically. We shared the very same headaches and shame on the outside and the same confusing and indescribable despair and doubts on the inside.

Support and new bonds of trust and camaraderie have been forming on and through this website's community for years now. I chose not to participate in any of the discussions largely because it took me months to process the overwhelming amount of information presented here, but it excited me. *I was suddenly NOT alone.* Sure, I knew of other hoarders and pack-rats, and their children, but I had NO idea – nor could I have ever imagined – the impact the hoard had on me…on us…mentally and emotionally.

Perhaps the one thing that surprised and fascinated me most was the correlation between an adult child of a hoarder and an adult child of an alcoholic.

My husband is an addictions counselor, and has not only been studying drugs and alcohol professionally, but he is also about to finish his graduate work in counseling psychology. He wrote a short paper hypothesizing hoarding as an addiction, rather than its current sub-classification under Obsessive-Compulsive Disorder. He presented some compelling arguments that might make one consider hoarding to be a type of addiction. In the end, he more or less concluded that it is likely not a subset of addiction, but it *could* be under a broader definition of "addiction." The interesting thing about this idea is that the psychological damage that severe hoarding and alcoholism both have on children, as revealed in their adulthood, are astonishingly similar.

Children of Hoarders shared a list of characteristics of adult children of alcoholics that could also be exhibited by people in my shoes. The following list is not all-inclusive, and is not in any particular order, but they are the traits I can personally relate to:

Characteristics of Adult Children of Alcoholics (ALCOA):
- Constantly seeking the approval of others
- An overdeveloped sense of responsibility
- Feelings of guilt associated with standing up for your rights
- Tendency to confuse feelings of love and pity
- Avoidance of feelings related to traumatic childhood experiences
- Low self-esteem
- Terrified of abandonment. Will do almost anything to hold onto a relationship.
- Dysfunctional relationships. Poor coping.
- Tendency to react to things that happen versus taking control and not being the victim

Clinical psychologist Steve Frisch, Psy.D. also notes some core issues these individuals regularly face and must make a conscious effort to overcome.

Core Issues:
- The fear of loss of control
- Trust
- Avoidance of feelings
- Over-responsibility ("model child")
- Ignore their own needs: "Feeling vulnerable also is equated with being out of control – a state of being which an ALCOA finds intolerable…forever in debt to the person who met their needs."

Then there's shame. Oh, the shame! Charles L. Whitfield, M.D., physician and psychotherapist renowned for his work with trauma victims, states, "In addition to feeling defective or inadequate, shame makes us believe that others can see through us, through our façade, into our defectiveness [...] We feel isolated and lonely with our shame, as though we are the only one who has the feeling." Feelings and actions that may mask our shame include anger, resentment, blame, rage, contempt, attack, control, perfectionism, neglect or withdrawal, abandonment, disappointment, compulsive behavior. I can absolutely identify with all of this.

So what causes hoarding? Is it genetic? Recent research suggests it is possible, if not probable. I was led to all of the following information through the aforementioned Children of Hoarders website.

The International OCD Foundation Hoarding website states, "From the earliest studies of hoarding, it has been clear that hoarding runs in families. Studies asking about family members have reported that 50 to 80% of people who hoard had first-degree relatives whom they considered 'pack rats' or hoarders. In a more stringent test of the family connection, the Johns Hopkins OCD Family Study diagnosed hoarding in 12% of first-degree relatives of people who hoarded. Although lower than the self-reported frequency found in other studies, it was still significantly greater than that of relatives of people with OCD (3%). Other studies have found evidence indicating that hoarding is genetically influenced."

Sanjaya Saxena, M.D., Director of the University of California, San Diego Obsessive-Compulsive Disorders Program, says in one of her letters to the editor of the *American Journal of Psychiatry*:

> "The OCD Collaborative Genetics Study is the third study to find genetic markers specifically associated with compulsive hoarding, indicating that it is a distinct and heritable phenotype. Other studies have confirmed that compulsive hoarding is strongly familial and appears to breed true."

In another letter she says:

> "Genetic and family studies suggest that compulsive hoarding has a different pattern of genetic inheritance and comorbidity (coexisting illnesses) than other OCD symptom factors. The hoarding/saving symptom factor has a recessive inheritance pattern, whereas the aggressive/checking and symmetry/order symptom factors show a dominant pattern."

Saxena goes on to describe detailed results of one study that demonstrate how "the hoarding/saving symptom factor was significantly associated with genetic markers" on three separate chromosomes. She also references a study whose findings showed that 84% of "OCD patients with prominent compulsive hoarding reported a family history of hoarding behaviors." Eight-four percent. That's huge!

Human chromosomes were also examined in an OCD Collaborative Genetics Study conducted by the Department of Psychiatry and Behavioral Sciences at Johns Hopkins University School of Medicine in March of 2007. Their findings suggest that a region on a fourth different chromosome is linked with compulsive hoarding behavior in families with OCD. To further elaborate, Randy O. Frost, PhD, says in the Spring 2007 New England Hoarding Consortium Newsletter:

> "In our first studies of hoarding we noticed a trend for this syndrome to run in families. Since then three genetics studies have appeared in the research literature, all suggesting that hoarding may be at least partly heritable. These studies start with select populations, like Tourette's patients or OCD patients, and look for people who hoard.
>
> One of these studies was done by the OCD Collaborative Genetics Study under the direction of investigators at the Johns Hopkins University Medical School. They found preliminary evidence that the genetic contribution to hoarding could be localized to a specific chromosome on the DNA chain. Something at chromosome 14 may be associated with hoarding. This could be a dramatic breakthrough in our understanding of hoarding.
>
> However, it is important to note that these studies are all preliminary with relatively small samples that don't fully represent the range of hoarding in the population. Furthermore, we also don't yet understand just what traits might be heritable. Perhaps it is something that underlies hoarding, like decision-making problems, and not hoarding itself that is inherited.
>
> To more fully determine the heritability of hoarding a much larger study is needed, one drawn from the entire population of people who hoard. That is, the sample must represent all people with hoarding problems and not just those who are already diagnosed with OCD. To that end, we have joined forces with the Johns Hopkins group to study the genetics of hoarding. Our first attempt to obtain funds from the National Institute of Mental Health (NIMH) for the project failed, but we will be trying again shortly.
>
> At this point we have no markers for the development of hoarding. We don't know who will and who won't develop hoarding problems. The best

advice we can give is to be open and honest with your children as they grow up about hoarding tendencies in the family. People who can recognize and talk about their own hoarding problems are much better able to control them than people who can't."

Several other studies have found evidence that links genetics to compulsive hoarding, including one conducted by researchers from King's College in London. Observing symptoms of hoarding in both fraternal and identical twins, David Mataix-Cols, Ph.D. and his team were able to isolate their results from "environmental factors," suggesting that hoarding is more innate than learned; but often there exists some outside "stressor" that instigates the real hoarding. A 2009 Reuters article covering this study notes that "Past research has shown that many people with hoarding problems have a history of traumatic events, according to Mataix-Cols." The most common traumatic events linked to hoarding include significant loss in the form of death or abandonment or even the loss of a home. In my mother's case, her mom, her cat, and her older sister all died; her purse was stolen at work; then I went (far) away to college – this all occurred within a ten-year time span. To say she experienced some loss that probably contributed to her *need* to hang on to things would be nothing less than accurate. In the same study, Mataix-Cols goes on to say that more research is necessary, and hopefully more effective treatment for compulsive hoarding will be found, "as behavioral therapy and antidepressants are now the main forms of treatment, but they have met with limited success."

Finally, David Tolin, PhD, ABPP (Founder and Director of the Anxiety Disorders Center, Director of the Division of Neuropsychology, Director of Health Psychology, and Director for Cognitive Behavioral Therapy at The Institute of Living) weighs in with some encouraging insight, in response to the possibility that a person may be predisposed to compulsive hoarding. Says Tolin, "For a condition like compulsive hoarding to come about you probably have to have a person who has a certain set of inherited characteristics, then that person then has to in some way learn or pick up the behavioral pattern. In other words, a person who naturally tends to be messy or even hoard CAN overcome. He adds, most vitally, "Biology is not destiny. Just because somebody has a genetic predisposition to develop a certain behavioral condition, that doesn't mean they are doomed." What a positive outlook to apply not only to hoarding, but to life in general!

If you are a child of a hoarder, know someone who is, or just want to learn more, I strongly encourage you to explore the Children of Hoarders website as a starting point. Its vast wealth of research, articles, discussion boards, and other helpful resources will take time to sift through, but you will not regret visiting. It will open your eyes! I certainly do not have all the answers, even having personally lived through it all, but I hope some of this information is useful or somehow encouraging to anyone in need of it, at least.

VALIDATE ME!

Chapter 6: Boys

Boy: "I like you."
Me: "Not. Say it again."
Boy: "I like you!"
Me: "I don't believe you. Write it down 20 times."

I think I was in sixth grade when I had this vain conversation with one boy, and it thrilled me to a hot blush when he handed me that paper. Not that it mattered; it was not as if we were going to date each other at eleven years old. I just got high off the power I thought I had over him for that brief week or so that he showed an interest in me – especially since he was kind of a punk, and I could not stand him prior to then.

Apparently I was kind of a punk, too – but more in the I-like-you-so-I'm-going-to-bug-the-crap-out-of-you way. I used to run around the playground literally chasing boys all the time, kicking them and teasing them, and just making my presence known. I was boy-crazy from a very young age. The first crush I can remember was a red-haired *Haole* boy in my preschool class. I think his name was Andy. After that, I recall major crushes on one of my dad's friends and one of my teachers – whose wife I evidently told I would steal him away from when I was about six years old. (She made sure to share this with me in front of my friends when we were older. Oh, I wouldn't live that down!) From then on, it is impossible to keep track, but I can probably still name at least one crush for every year of my young life.

In seventh grade, at the height of my awkwardness thanks to puberty (complete with acne and braces), the crushes got out of control. In the midst of my hormones-run-wild emotions for every other guy, I fell excessively hard for someone that I wound up pursuing for three desperately confusing and painful years. I had never felt that way about anyone before, and in my foolish naïveté, was convinced I was in love. It was entirely one-sided, but I persevered, believing that "good things come to those who wait" and doing anything I could to grab his attention without looking like an idiot.

We were friends, but it was an odd friendship. I never really knew where I stood with him, and was always too insecure to just enjoy his company, whether on the phone or in person. Most of our phone conversations were silent. He would call me (for a while it was daily), we would exchange greetings and formalities, and then no one would talk for 30 minutes. If I thought of something, I would ask or comment, but the majority of the call was dead air. While I am certain he was just sitting there reading magazines or playing video games or something, and could not have cared less, I was on the other end gritting my teeth and mentally freaking out.

I would think to myself every five minutes or so, *"Say something interesting or funny! Don't bore him! He's going to hang up and never call again! Show him you're fun to be with! Ask him who he likes! NO, don't do that...you asked him last week. Compliment him! Ask him what he is doing right now..."* I would try to get some mindless homework done during the awkward silence, but I would drop everything and hang onto every word if he spoke. I never understood why we did that. *Did he like my mere presence? Was he playing mind games with me?* Whatever it was, I got used to it, and when it became less frequent and eventually stopped, I questioned everything. *What did I do? Did I say something stupid? Is he mad at me? Why doesn't he like me?*

It always came back to that final, unanswerable, gut-wrenching question. (He would later inform me that he thought I was cute and smart but not his type.)

As asinine as it was, I latched on to him because of the attention he gave me, even if it was not much. (As it turns out, I did this with my female and older friends, too.) I became obsessed with him, keeping everything he ever gave me or that reminded me of him – a card, drawings on my textbook cover, a quiz he graded, a string from his backpack, an attendance roster with his name on it... I tortured my friends with regular declarations of my love for him, and wrote "I 'heart' (his name)" on everything. I wrote poems for him, dedicated songs to him, cried over him, and constantly pleaded with God that he would like me. Once, I went out of my way to help him with a project; another time, I spent weeks of my allowance to buy him a PlayStation memory card because he said he needed one and jokingly asked me to get it for him. I tried to impress his friends, and even got fairly close to one of them for a while. I did not stalk him (I couldn't drive yet), but if my parents and I ever happened to be near his neighborhood, I would ask them to take a certain route home so I could catch a glimpse of his house from the road. I got jealous when I saw him smiling at or laughing with other girls. It was all so very pathetic.

I briefly dated someone else in eighth grade – my first "official" boyfriend – but once that was over, the crush resumed with full force. And I was convinced I would somehow win him over one day. At one point during our freshman year, we actually hung out a couple times in a small group. At our Spring Banquet, we sat at the same table and took photos together (again, in a group). It was one of the best nights of my life. I barely spoke to him, of course, but I do remember smiling and laughing a lot. That whole year was amazing because of him. Then, all of a sudden, he drifted away. *Did I scare him off? Did he think we were getting too close?*

The following year I got more heavily involved in extracurricular activities, so my idle time spent obsessing over him quickly became nonexistent, we talked less and less, and I started getting to know other guys. My feelings for him started gradually and naturally fading. When he started dating someone and then ultimately transferred schools, things got easier for me to let go of him. I still thought he was gorgeous, and treasured all the memories fondly, but I was relieved to finally move on.

My sophomore year of high school, the hottest guy in school took me to our Spring Banquet. He was the school heartthrob, and I had never felt more validated by a guy, due entirely to the attention I received from him. He chose ME over all the girls lined up for him! I was a nervous wreck the entire time, shaking as I pinned the boutonnière to his jacket, sweating during our photos, and being uncharacteristically shy and practically mute the rest of the night. He was a perfect gentleman, and was almost as quiet, but the pressure I put upon myself to be pretty and amazing and interesting that evening was so obvious that it detracted from my inner euphoria and no doubt made him uncomfortable. Sigh... So much for that. We were still friends after that, but never anything more. I sometimes wondered what would have happened if he had not moved away. Maybe we would have dated, and I would have calmed down…or maybe I would just have ruined it. I was just so awkward.

If there were one thing I was consistently good at, in general, it was focusing on the negative, tainting an otherwise perfect situation or encounter. I still catch myself doing that from time to time, but becoming conscious of this fault has helped me prevent a total eclipse of all things positive. Growing up and experiencing REAL heartache and loss in more recent years have also allowed me to gain some valuable perspective on life as a whole.

I also got the obsessing thing down pat. The aforementioned three-year crush wasn't the only one that afflicted me to the core; it was just the first of many. But even if there were no real feelings associated, it was common for me to even just obsess over a particular aspect of a cute guy, such as his cologne. The scent of one such guy was intoxicating and I actually developed an attraction to the guy wearing it solely because of it. After that caught my attention, I noticed he also had nice eyes and I liked his voice; but if not for the cologne, I probably would have never looked at him in "that way." I ended up carrying around a sample card thingy of that cologne in my wallet for years and asked three subsequent boyfriends to wear that specific scent when I was with them. Not because it reminded me of the first guy…just because something about it turned me on.

On two separate occasions, I befriended guys to talk up my girl friends who had crushes on them, and try to set them up, only to discover later that the guys were interested in me. The first time that happened, I tried to resist in the name of loyal friendship, but ultimately wound up dating the guy for a year. Not surprisingly, that friendship was never the same after that, and I was a rather jealous girlfriend. (Feeling guilty much?) It was not uncommon for me to become immediately interested in someone once I learned of their attraction to me. THAT happened way, way more times than I care to admit.

But even when I was in a relationship, I craved and sought the attention or affection of other boys, knowing full well nothing would or could ever come of it. I was often called a tease because I would flirt with a guy, but then slowly become disinterested when he started to like me. I certainly never meant any harm. I didn't do these things intentionally. I didn't even know why I was like that. I just liked the attention. It made me feel good. I was often interested in more than one guy at a time, and I *always* had to be actively attracted to someone. When I was not naturally feeling anything toward anyone for a while, I deliberately sought my next object of affection. Like a hungry lion, searching for its prey! Yes, part of that was attributed to my out-of-control adolescent hormones, but what more than that?

I was also guilty of eating up the attention of guys who were interested in me, but who I had zero interest in. It's not that I found them repulsive, they just weren't my type. I badly broke the hearts of at least three boys in high school, one of whom I actually did try to date for a couple of months. I did not WANT to hurt them, and was genuinely sorry that I did; but in my excitement of knowing they liked me, let alone noticed me at all, I innocently gave off the wrong signals, making them think they had a chance. And by "signals," I mean smiling while talking to them, accepting a rose on Valentine's Day, or going for a moonlit stroll to talk about deep, philosophical stuff. Again, I had no intention of misleading anyone. Unfortunately, two of those three incidents created some nasty enemies. I received anonymous threats online over Instant Messenger, I was tipped off that someone almost slashed my tires while I was at work, and several mutual friends completely stopped talking to me and started gossiping behind my back – all after I had tried to be as gentle and humble as possible when informing them I simply was not interested in being more than friends.

Looking back, I realize I had an issue with boundaries. I let myself get closer to or was friendlier with the opposite gender than perhaps I should have been. I was not physically intimate with any of them; then again, that was not what I lacked. I craved attention. Affection. Approval. Validation. I had no idea that I was actually hurting people in the process of so desperately seeking what I did not even realize I needed.

In 2001, I entered a relationship with a guy I had casually "met" online in a chat room about four years prior. We had lost touch, and life went on; then out of the blue one day, we reconnected. He was in New York, and I was in Hawai`i, but I was on my way to college in Pennsylvania. We thought it was destiny. I was completely infatuated with him. Besides being super sweet and romantic and incredibly good-looking, we seemed to share a similar moral code. We spent hours, late into the night (across time zones, which was tricky), video chatting, flirting, and eventually falling for each other. We had no idea what we were doing, or where this was going.

I remained single by choice throughout my senior year of high school, certain that he and I would end up together when I went to college. But mostly, I had done the long-distance thing before and hated it, so I did not want to endure that again. In the meantime, however, I was still sixteen. By no means was I wild, except with my heart. I fell for a tall, incredibly gorgeous, funny, sweet Christian guy I worked with at my part-time job, who was interested in me and *was* open to a long-distance relationship. It pained me to say no to him. I wanted him so badly! Another friend and I got rather close just before graduation, and we kind of made the old If-we're-still-single-when-we're-30 pact. Oh, and let us not forget how boy-crazy I went on our senior trip to California, surrounded by nice-looking guys, every one of which reminded me of my very own, who was waiting for me in New York.

I stuck to my guns, though, and saved my heart for him. My mom and I stayed in New York City with one of her friends for a couple weeks before my college life commenced. A couple days before move-in day, she and I took a train up to meet him and his family. Within an hour or so, we were holding hands, and officially dating. It was highly-anticipated, new, and exhilarating. It did not take long for us to say the L-word to each other.

But I was still so young and jealous. I felt myself seethe with envy as he told me about the one other girl from his past that he had kissed, even though I was his first real girlfriend. He was a year younger than me, and had less experience with dating relationships. And even though we had communicated online a lot and felt like we had known each other forever by the time we did start dating, things did move pretty fast. As it turned out, he was prone to jealousy, too. We got into our first real argument at my freshman year Homecoming dance, about two months into the relationship. Something just was not right, and I was not happy. I know I should have ended it then, before we got too invested in one another, but I am stubborn and loyal to a fault, and rarely a quitter, and we agreed that this was just a "test of our love" that we would get through and come out stronger as a result.

I cannot tell you how many things I should have NOT stuck with over the years. In hindsight, my "loyalty" held me back from many growth opportunities, both personal and professional. In this particular case, I think the core reason I held on was fear – the fear of not meeting another guy, mostly.

Anyway, we both seemed to be jealous types, but I quickly started to feel less like a girlfriend and more like a possession. For the first year, he still lived in New York, so we took turns traveling by train (4 trains and 2 subways, to be exact) to visit each other during long weekends and breaks. It was an adventure, and I really did not mind. I enjoyed being with him, and missed him terribly when we were apart. After he graduated from high school, he moved about a half an hour away from me, which was awesome because we were able to see each other whenever we wanted, but at least every weekend. The thing is, that seemed to become the expectation, and if I ever wanted to do something different or without him (i.e. go home with my roommate), I felt incredibly guilty about it. At first it was cute; I felt wanted, needed, loved. After a while, though, I felt suffocated. We started fighting constantly, over everything and anything. He especially did not like it when I talked to or hung out with my guy friends, and once called me a whore because I was not willing to shun them for his sake. (Side note: I can assure you that there was no whoring occurring at any point in my life, ever.)

And yet, we persevered…for three long, confusing years. We had our good times, many laughs and inside jokes that I can still recall today, some that still make me smile. I embraced his culture and purposely learned his language to deeper assimilate into it – though that was not enough to impress his mother! When I told her I was minoring in their language, she muttered under her breath, "Yeah, right." Perhaps it was my broken perception at the time, but it seemed his family never really did fully accept me. I think his siblings genuinely tried to – we got along, at least – but his mom always thought the worst of me, and of us as a couple. She would *constantly* go off at him in front of me (usually loudly, sometimes in their language) about how she would not tolerate sex in her house, despite our insistence that we were not having sex (we weren't). One morning when I was staying with them, I silently stumbled into the kitchen, and before I had a chance to say anything, she startled me with an irritated "Good MORNING, Melissa," and when I responded, "Oh, good morning," she retorted to my equally-surprised boyfriend, "WELL, she didn't say nothing to ME!" I will give him credit in that he tried to defend me, and us as a couple, many times, but I was justifiably uneasy at the prospect of becoming a part of his family. Still, I kept putting on a happy face because I wanted to be accepted by them.

In the end, I grew resentful of it all, especially him. The "love" was long gone, and I could barely stand to look at him anymore. I felt emotionally abused, and foresaw a marriage with him full of bitterness, betrayal, and hurt. By the time we broke up, my heart had already moved on, and there was no question that we were not going to make it work.

It was one of the most detrimental, toxic relationships I have ever endured by choice, largely because I let myself believe that he was the only one who would ever want me. For years following our break-up, I blamed him for destroying what little self-esteem I had left, or brainwashing me into thinking I was worthless. But it was ME. Yes, he said some horrible things to me in the heat of the moment (I'm sure I did, too). Yes, I felt smothered and discouraged from pursuing my own interests and goals. I was just too scared to leave, for fear of not being accepted by the next guy. *I was scared of starting over.* How many more guys would have to find out about my parents' house? That's not really all it was about, but I did despise sharing that part of me with people. I learned a lot of important lessons through it all, but I ultimately saw it as three wasted years – wasted money, wasted tears, wasted time – and I could have walked away at Homecoming. Call it young love, naïveté, or foolishness, but something deeper in me kept me holding on. As crappy as things were, I had a cute boyfriend! Someone accepted me. Could I have gotten other guys? Maybe. I didn't entertain that thought while I was with him, but I certainly had options. True to my boy-crazy habits, I did let my eyes wander a bit when things got rough with him, and had my share of innocent, completely one-sided, secret crushes on other guys throughout our relationship. It was not until the end that I finally gave in and acted on one of them.

In early 2003, I was working at a coffee shop, my second part-time job, when I met Billy – or Bill as I first knew him. Billy did not impress me at first. I thought he was very arrogant, and I could not stand the way he did certain things. (To be fair, he wasn't my biggest fan either!) A few months after he joined our store, I found out he was a Christian, like me. I thought it was interesting to have that in common with him, and we slowly started warming up to each other. Eventually, I learned he was in a rough relationship, like I was.

Our store kicked off every Christmas season with a holiday meeting, during which we would learn about all the special offerings, taste new coffees and treats, and just have fun together as a team. I walked in as I was furiously cutting short argument number 43239582813 with my boyfriend, as the meeting was going to start soon, and I was visibly very upset. Billy was the only one who saw me when I hung up, and asked if I was OK. *The jerk cared?* Apparently he did, and not long after, we began to form a friendship. He was there for me, and I was there for him. Sometimes we would sit in the parking lot after we closed the store, just chatting about life and relationships. I started to think he was kind of cute, too.

Spring Break of my junior year (2004), my boyfriend and I went to Ireland, just for fun. I had become inexplicably obsessed with the country and found a way to make the 8-day trip affordable for us. I think he knew in his heart, as much as I did, that we were not going to be together much longer; but the trip was booked months in advance, so we went anyway and tried to make the most of it. On one of our last nights, over dinner, he started talking about celebrities and asked which ones I found attractive. I felt interrogated and refused to answer him. Up to this point, I had become so paranoid about relating to other guys that I trained myself to say, "I don't notice anyone but you." The subject was dropped, only to be quickly followed by a presumption that I was going to break up with him. In an effort to enjoy what was left of our trip, I urged him to let it go.

"Let's not ruin the trip. We can talk about all that when we get home."
"No, if you're going to break up with me, just do it. Why wait?"

Finally, after going back and forth for a while, he made the decision and broke up with me. He did not speak to me the rest of the night, or the following day, or on the flight home. When we finally landed in Philly, we learned that the airline had lost our luggage. (We had changed planes in Baltimore. Upon our arrival, we identified our bags before getting on the ever-loathed domestic carrier that shall again remain nameless. Our bags made it across the freaking Atlantic, but couldn't make it from Baltimore to Philly? Sigh.) Before we got that news, we sat staring at the baggage claim conveyor belts for almost an hour. In silence. Oh, except for when he erroneously thought I was looking at some random guy, and questioned why I was doing that. Of course he did not believe me when I said, "What guy? I haven't taken my eyes off the stupid conveyor belt since we sat down!" (It was the truth.)

Once we found out that our bags did not make it, we took a train from the airport into the city, where I figured we were parting ways for the night. Apparently, after a break-up and two days of not speaking except to make a false accusation against me, he still thought I would go with him to his apartment, and was at first hurt but then angry that I vehemently refused. Honestly, as disgusted as I was with him, I did not go because I did not trust myself. I doubted how strong I would be if I did go with him, fearful that we would somehow work things out, or he would talk me into starting over. But I was done. It took a lot of will-power for me to walk away, but I had to.

As soon as I got back to campus, I called Billy to inform him that I was back and I was single. Within days, he was single, too. My now-ex-boyfriend tried to get back together more than once after all this – once, showing up on- unannounced. We talked a little, but I told him I had moved on. I would have to see him one more time a few weeks later to settle some business with our cell phones, and we would talk briefly a couple times thereafter, but otherwise, he was out of my life.

A year later, shortly after I returned from a class trip to Buenos Aires, Billy and I were engaged. We have been happily married since June 2006.

I laugh whenever people ask where Billy and I met, because our story did not start out very romantically. It usually begins, "We worked at a coffee shop together…but we didn't really like each other at first." Yes, I came to find out – during my bridal shower, no less – that his first impression of me was "cute but annoying." I still don't like the way he does some things…but he is significantly humbler than when I first met him! Seriously though, he is a patient, loving, and thoughtful husband and father; he has seen me AND my parents at our very worst; he has been supportive through my therapeutic journey; and it is abundantly clear that he was the right choice for me in the end.

That is not to say we have had a perfect, fairytale romance. One does not usually drop a lifetime of baggage in the blink of an eye and start over like nothing ever happened. I was screwed up, but...Billy loved me anyway. More importantly, I learned from all those past mistakes. I knew what I did NOT want in a relationship, and was determined to never let myself feel devalued again. That meant I was often on the defensive, and when something started to go wrong, or I did not get my way but felt justified in having it, I did not stand for it. I felt so free and empowered when I left my ex-boyfriend for Billy, which was a positive thing; but unchecked, it could have ruined a good thing. I have said some nasty things to him in anger that I never should have even thought, but I was ultimately humbled by Billy's grace toward me. I can't count the number of times I have asked him why he (still) loves me! But he does, and I am so grateful for his constant care and support. I do not take that for granted, ever.

Nowadays I am unable to tell if a guy is interested in me or has a crush on me. I know, I know – I'm married, so it should not matter. And it truly does not matter, but let's be honest: It IS nice to know you've still got it going on! Seriously, though, no matter what signs a guy might throw at me, I *never* assume he is into me. I am not oblivious; I just disregard or distrust any signs I might notice.

There has been one person in the last seven years to admit he had a crush on me, and even then, I did not believe him at first. When I finally did believe him, I just thought he was nuts. I was only ever asked for my phone number by a complete stranger once in my life, and half of the few relationships I have been in were somewhat set up by the meddling of friends. I have never been one to put myself in situations to expose myself to single men (bars and clubs, for instance, are just not my scene), and I will always be polite (i.e. thank a gentleman for holding a door for me), but will generally mind my own business and not make eye contact with people I do not know. Would I act otherwise if I were single? Perhaps, but I think a part of me simply became overprotective of myself over the years. I find it easier to be friendly with men than women, however, which is always how I have been, and many of the women I know say the same thing. I have been called "intimidating," with or without my wedding ring, and that has always upset me because I try to appear approachable. Maybe it's the eye contact thing...

In any case, I have found myself in a dichotomy here – giving off an air of disinterest (Defense mechanism? Overcompensation?) yet yearning to feel liked and accepted by everyone. The problem with my spending all of my energy trying to be accepted is that I never learned how to accept myself. I set myself up for failure from the start by placing unreasonable expectations upon myself – and others. This did nothing to foster my self-esteem. As a result, I never believed people when they complimented me, I never thought I had any real talents, and I never spoke up for myself. I have started to improve in all of these areas, but the one thing I continue to struggle with is how others see me, especially when they are not blatant or vocal with their opinions.

My default assumption is that people do not like me, or that I am annoying. I admit, once I open up to people, I can talk too much, and I even start to annoy myself; but I am acutely conscious of this in every setting and will quickly cut myself off if I notice the other person losing interest. I do tend to be able to read people well, but I am not always right. My challenge, then, becomes not getting defensive. I have been guilty of throwing pity parties (fishing for some verbal affirmation, perhaps?), which I cannot stand about myself! I have been trying to stop myself from saying, "I can tell you're bored...sorry, I'll shut up now," or the like, because, inevitably, the person gets embarrassed – if not for him/herself, then for me – and wants to be nice; and whether or not s/he is bored, will say, "Oh, no! Sorry, I'm just tired. I'm interested!" And then I get all paranoid and usually don't want to keep talking anymore out of sheer awkwardness. I have to not care about that so much.

The fact is, I do gauge the interest level, and I'm really not trying to come across as self-absorbed. I know this, so I shouldn't worry about someone not liking me just because I get chatty at times. By itself that is a pretty silly reason to not like someone, and I have to give my friends the benefit of the doubt that they are more civil and gracious than that.

That said, I am relieved to not be single and in pursuit of a mate. I would not even know how to handle it.

Chapter 7: Normal

"I'm not where I need to be, but thank God I'm not where I used to be. I'm OK, and I'm on my way!" – Joyce Meyer

* * *

Let me pause for a moment and acknowledge the unquestionable fact that I was and still am immensely blessed beyond measure, knowing full well that my circumstances growing up could have been unimaginably worse. Despite the lack of proper emotional nurturing and despite undesirable living conditions, I do have SO many happy memories. I know I started to get bitter as I got older, but I am forever grateful that I did not feel compelled to withdraw into a reclusive lifestyle or seek temporary solace in dangerous behaviors, such as drugs or alcohol.

(Side note: If you are struggling with something – anything – I urge you to seek help. You CAN overcome whatever is hurting or otherwise affecting you. Please take care of yourself, and do not give up. No matter what you have done or what anyone else has told you to the contrary, you are worth it. I promise!)

All along the way I did always try to make the most of my situation, and although I was secretive about my house, I have always been open about mostly everything else, including my closeness with my parents. I was not any more embarrassed of them than the average teenager might be, and I told them pretty much everything. They knew who my friends were, they knew about every single crush, they knew if I bombed a quiz or had a disagreement with a teacher, etc. All things being equal, our relationship was normal – at least it felt that way to me. Not perfect, but usually OK, and certainly far from bad or scary.

Yet it is almost as if something inside me was programmed to prevent me from feeling happy. I do not know when that started, or what triggered it, but I have always had a knack for finding the cloud inside the silver lining. I bounced back and forth between calling myself a pessimist and realist, but the one undeniable truth was that I was petty. I was often easily annoyed about the smallest, stupidest stuff.

It pushed friends away, made me appear unapproachable, and led people to walk on eggshells around me. I finally caught on and, frankly, got aggravated with myself, realizing I just needed to chill the heck out! It took most of my life, though, to recognize how NOT normal my life was, and that I would not be able to heal on my own. Accepting this realization was a crucial first step to finding a new normal.

Time and experience slowly taught me what really mattered, and helped me truly comprehend and accept that things could always be worse. Everyone has their own battles. God obviously knew that I could not handle an alcoholic father or a physical handicap, so He gave the strength to endure a hoarding mother. If only I had known sooner how this would shape me in the years to come!

I see it all clearly now, and for that I am beyond grateful. I cannot imagine the person I would be in ten or twenty years if I had continued down the same path I was headed down and not received help. What a lonely, bitter life I would have brought upon myself!

It was not just therapy, though, that "saved" me from myself. Having my first child softened me. I became a different person the moment she was in my arms. I used to be hard, unforgiving, spiteful, and somewhat uncompassionate. A lot of it was linked to my childhood, but that needed to change. That's no way for anyone to live. A couple years after she was born, the end of a special friendship broke me and whatever was left of my pride. It was one of the worst pains I had known, but I eventually understood that it had to happen for both our sakes, and I chose to grow and learn from it. Now I think before I speak. I am slower to judge and I try to understand both sides of an issue before jumping to conclusions. I see the world through very different eyes today.

Also along the way, friends of ours nearly lost their precious little boy – twice – to cancer. Their struggle, a parent's worst nightmare, gave me real perspective for the first time in my adult life. Through his tragedy, and way too many others close to home (bombings, school shootings, stories of child abuse and molestation, etc.), it became easier to NOT feel sorry for myself. I believe whenever you are hurt you still have to go through the stages of grief or loss to effectively heal, which I did. I personally believe that it is OK to wallow quietly for a moment, but at some point, you end the pity party, gain that perspective, and then it stops being all about you. You refocus and remind yourself of your true purpose – or gain a new one.

Sometimes repeating the word "Perspective" over and over, like a mantra, was the only thing that got me through the bad days. That, and prayer – just a simple, "Take this pain, God. Please just take it." I HATE that it took a series of loss and tragedies to get my attention, but I was too self-centered to see past my own pain. That is also not a way for anyone to live.

I still struggle with my self-esteem today, but just as I cannot expect my mother's years of hoarding to stop overnight, I am learning to be patient with myself. It takes time to relearn and retrain your mind, but with discipline and the support of positive influences around you, you will find that it is possible. No matter what has happened in the past, tomorrow is a new day, and another chance to build (or rebuild) your self-image to a healthy level that allows you to do much more than just function – but to LIVE and LOVE and serve others. We all have scars, some more painful than others. Mine are relational, and the reason I handled so much of that dysfunctionally was because I knew of no other way.

I have a history of letting people take advantage of me that goes back to at least elementary school. When I was in gymnastics, there was this one girl I wanted to be friends with. Even though she was a few years younger than me, she was the niece of the owner, and was pretty and popular – and also kind of mean to me at first. One day, on the first day of ballet training, which we sometimes did to enrich our movement, she realized she had forgotten her ballet slippers. When she saw my brand-spanking-new, white slippers, she begged to borrow them. (She probably threw in the old, "I'll be your best friend!" line that we were all guilty of using and naïvely believing at that age.) I was so desperate for acceptance that I let her use them. She got them so filthy that my parents were furious with me for letting someone else wear them. When she saw them scolding me, she felt bad for me and from then on, she was my friend for several years until we lost touch when I went away to college.

In third grade, my best friend at the time hosted a sleepover with some other girls and me. She had a reputation of being bossy, but again, she was popular and had lots of nice things…and she called herself my best friend, which was hugely validating for an eight-year-old only child with an odd home life. I don't remember much about that night except when it was getting close to bedtime. I recall her making me go to sleep before everyone else, without explanation, and then demanding that I wake up in the middle of the night to clean her room or the bathroom, or something like that. I remember lying in the bed with the blanket over my head, feeling humiliated, and pretending to sleep. One of our friends whispered to me, "It's OK," which received a reprimand to not speak to me. I know I had done nothing to deserve such a punishment. I don't know if it was because I was half-Caucasian during a phase when my non-Caucasian friends were oddly preoccupied by race. Who knows? Whatever the reason, she was a bully to me, and I took it from her because, once again, I desired little else but acceptance.

In seventh grade, I entered a new school. A bunch of kids transferred there from my elementary school, so I did know some people; but I had spent most of my elementary years with girls who ended up going to different schools, so I essentially had to start over. For reasons unknown, one cute, perky girl in my class quickly took me under her wing and showed me the ropes. When she left the school after eighth grade, she was just as quick to betray me (again, for reasons unknown) and the friendship we had in between was more often than not uncomfortable. She was the type of friend who did not want you to wear the same type of clothes as her or have the same hairstyle or generally like the same stuff she did. I was terrified to tell her that she had gotten me into Sailor Moon – and that I watched it every day after school – for fear of what she might say or do. She often exaggerated stories, but no matter how blatantly I knew she was lying, I never called her out on it. She told me we were best friends, and I did not want to lose that. I was always apologizing for everything, even when I knew I did nothing wrong.

In eighth grade, a good friend and I started going to church and youth group together. She and I never found our place amongst those youth, however, being the only "private school kids" in the bunch, dressing more conservatively than the other girls, and not showing interest in the gossip and other topics of discussion outside of the Bible study itself. The few kids that did talk to us as well as all the leaders were nice to us, but we were otherwise outcasts in an environment that should have been positive and accepting. We kept going to church but eventually stopped attending the youth group because there was no point. At that age, when you are trying to fit in while simultaneously figuring out who you are, it can be difficult to stand up for yourself. There is only so much a person can take.

I have many other examples like these that I do not share to make you feel sorry for me, but rather, to further illustrate my desperate need for validation in whatever way I could get it. Even if there were no bullying involved, the *absence* of that validation was just as damaging.

During my senior year of college and shortly after that, my husband, who I was dating at the time, became a huge part of my life and we spent a lot of time with his friends in the area. It was most likely unintentional, but quite often a couple of his friends used to make me feel like a loser. Every time we would hang out with them, they would call me "weird," and sometimes Billy would say in jest, "I don't know what's wrong with her" or "she's crazy" whenever I would say something silly or funny, rather than just laugh. This happened repeatedly until I ultimately stopped enjoying spending time with them. They were (are) good people, offered a ton of help and advice, and we did have some fun over the years, but I got along with them best when we were discussing a serious subject. Other than that, I felt like the butt of the joke for the night. It wasn't that I didn't have a sense of humor – I make fun of myself all the time – and it's not like they sat around bashing me the whole time, either. The problem was, the teasing was rarely offset by any praise or positive talk about me (verbal affirmation). They showed concern when appropriate, but they never had anything nice to say about me – except that I was better than Billy's ex-girlfriend. Any lighthearted conversation demeaned me at some point along the way, or somehow made me feel like a misfit.

I was never comfortable enough with them to speak up, and Billy did not think these situations ever warranted defending me, so it never got addressed. More accurately, he was desensitized to it. At the time, I did not appreciate any kind of teasing or mockery as a form of endearment or as an appropriate part of a friendship, but he had grown used to it with them. I have since learned to recognize that, when done in good fun, some people do this when they actually like someone. I doubt they had even realized how much it bothered me, because I sometimes laughed to cover up my uneasiness, but eventually I just shut down. I never said much around them to begin with, having little in common with them, but it got to a point where I finally closed myself off to them completely. I was tired of feeling like crap whenever we left their house or apartment, no matter how hard I tried to fit in with them.

Verbal affirmation was craved the most amongst the older women in my life. I rarely received it growing up, and feel that I still do not receive it sufficiently, and once again, I allowed myself to be damaged by the absence of that validation.

Another way this plays out is that I feel useless when I am not asked for help or for my opinion, especially when someone knows I have knowledge on a particular subject. I have long assumed that I was just disregarded or forgotten about, but I am told more often than not that it is out of respect for my time and/or privacy. In other words, people didn't want to "bother" me. That disturbed me just the same because that implied I was giving off a vibe that I'm only concerned with myself. I have tried to be more conscious of my "resting b-face" over the years because I was told in the past that I "always look angry." In high school, a classmate once randomly gave me a note that said it was my choice to be mad at her and to please keep my comments to myself – which completely blindsided me because I was not mad at anybody, especially her. Yikes! What kind of persona was I displaying?

Some tell me I am intimidating, especially before you get to know me. I still do not fully understand that one. Maybe it's the way I wear my make-up? I say that because on the rare occasions that I have gone out bare-faced, people smile at me more. Maybe that is just a coincidence, but it is kind of funny! Seriously, though, I am a petite 5'2" and my default personality amongst strangers is calm and reserved. I can be loud and passionate and opinionated when I get into a heated discussion, am talkative in the company of friends, and can sometimes come across as high-strung when I'm energized, but until you really get to know me, I am actually more on the demure side and I try to mind my own business. I might not make eye contact with random people on the street, and I'm terrible at starting conversations, but I always acknowledge people who talk to me. While some might take the intimidation thing as a compliment, it always offended me.

Looking back at all the negative relationships in my life, I see now that I certainly did take some things too personally, internalizing way too much without appropriately addressing it. Perhaps if I had had a better attitude toward people overall, I would have found a way to get along better with them. Maybe they really didn't like me. OR maybe they did, they just didn't show it in MY way (the aforementioned love language argument). In any case, I should not have placed so much of my own self-worth upon my perception of how others perceived me.

I spent so much of my life bitter and judgmental until I started to see how each person really has his or her own story. The other day at church our pastor asked us to raise our hand if we have ever experienced fear. Before he even finished his question, a large, burly man – who some might ignorantly label as "scary" or "intimidating" – raised his hand. Our pastor said to hold on and wait until he read his list of circumstances that could induce fear. That brief, lighthearted moment elicited some chuckles, but I heard the guy say under his breath, "Everything," before that list was read. Eventually everyone's hands were raised, but that man made an impression on me. On the outside, someone who does not know this tough-looking dude would probably never guess that he feared anything. The point is, when we let go of preconceived notions and prejudices, it is a lot easier to see how we are all in this together. *Why do we discount this?*

Our pastor often says, "Hurt people hurt people." How I wish I had truly grasped the truth of that statement the first time I heard it years ago! I try to remind myself of this daily now, whenever I feel offended or insulted or when I witness emotional pain, humiliation, or insults inflicted on those around me. For most of my life, my natural response to abuse of any kind would be, "What a horrible person! How could anyone treat someone like that?" I am slowly learning to shift my response to, "I wonder what trauma that person experienced to become like that." Don't get me wrong, I still get incensed by any kind of injustice, especially toward those without a voice (such as children and animals), and I am still a strong proponent of administering fitting consequences; but my heart has finally started learning compassion, too.

Because hurt people do hurt people, we will continue to breed vengeful, vindictive generations until someone finally chooses to break that cycle. Until someone recognizes his or her own hurt, where it comes from, and starts to heal, s/he will hurt those around them – verbally, physically, emotionally, whatever.

Sometimes it is intentional, sometimes it is not. It is "easy" for an angry parent to raise an angry child, and for that angry child to raise an angry child, and so on. It is much harder work to control your anger and not teach it to your kids. Isn't it worth it, though? Break the cycle. That is something I am working on every single day. And every day I fall short in some way, but I am keeping myself in check and taking baby steps away from my old, angry self.

In the case of a child of a hoarder, it is not only imperative to break the cycle of hurt, but also the cycle of hoarding itself. We must learn the balance between not turning into an obsessive neat-freak and not turning into a hoarder.

At times I catch myself exhibiting mild hoarding tendencies. With food, I act as if it will be gone forever once I eat it all, and never be able to buy it again, so I make it last forever. In my defense, I really don't think it is THAT crazy for me to take my time consuming special items that are hard to come by, such as the goodies my parents send me from Hawai'i that you can only find there, or seasonal items. I once made a box of Girl Scout cookies last for 2 years (Thin Mints actually stay fresh in the fridge or freezer when they're sealed well!); but I have also been known to get down to the last box/can/container/bag/package of something, and not consume it until I have replenished my supply. I do that for a lot of household items, too. I dread running out of certain things, and I tend to stock up on stuff, but *within reason*. Where I really start to check myself is when I look at a nice empty box or container and think of uses for it. While I do keep a very small stash for gifts and shipping material, my rule is to throw it out if I can't think of a use for it immediately. "You can always find another box if you don't keep this one," I remind myself, and into recycling it goes without further thought. *I will NOT become a hoarder.*

Truth be told, I love trash day! A full garbage bag gives me an abnormal delight with which most people probably cannot identify. I also love donating huge bags of stuff to charity. I actually do not like to throw away things that someone could still find a legitimate use for, so I list it on Craigslist or Freecycle or I try to sell it if it is in good enough shape. I hate wasting anything, but I try not to keep things if they are doing nothing but taking up space. I keep a big tub in our attic as a "memory box" of sorts, full of cards, ticket stubs, playbills and programs, letters, and stuff from trips (maps, pamphlets, etc.), so I do appreciate sentimental value, but I contain it – quite literally.

The hoarding tendencies are not limited to keeping things, though. Author and fellow daughter-of-a-hoarder, Jessie Sholl, in her book *Dirty Secret* puts it best, and takes it a step further to touch on other non-materialistic characteristics hoarders display – all of which I have seen in myself. Says Sholl, "I'm more determined than ever to not end up like my mother. Given the strong genetic component to hoarding, sometimes I worry that the proclivity is within me, lying dormant, waiting for a catastrophe to set it in motion. I begin to mentally sift through my behavior, hoping that self-awareness will be the inoculation I need. I'm definitely not a hoarder in terms of possession, and it's not hard for me to keep things organized in our apartment. But I am really indecisive [...] Then there's my ridiculously bad sense of direction [...] I'm shy and prone to isolation the way my mother is, and I often have to force myself to make plans with people or go to a party. When I do, I'm always glad I did, but I have to remind myself to make the effort. My natural tendency is to stay inside and nest. And I'm a perfectionist, there's no question" (pp. 273-274). Exactly!

More often than not, now that I have a house to call my own, I tend to overcompensate for the past because I never want anyone to think I am inclined toward becoming a hoarder. The mail pile only gets tolerated for a couple of weeks, magazines are promptly recycled, empty disposable food containers and cups are immediately thrown away, the fridge gets cleaned out weekly, expired items are tossed, clothes we don't wear get donated, and – most notably – I go into a cleaning frenzy when people are coming over, even though my husband thinks the house looks fine. *I will NOT become a hoarder.*

When my parents come to visit, I am extra-careful to show my mother what a house is supposed to be like…as if it were my job, as if she doesn't already know. I do not want her to think even for a second that I am following in her footsteps. I do not want to appear condoning or hypocritical in any way, and I do not want to give her any ideas that she can take home with her. Sadly, I have seen my mom perpetuate her hoarding when she visits (suddenly an empty egg carton in the recycling bin winds up in the guest bedroom my parents are staying in). It infuriates me to see it happening before my eyes, in my own house, but her resources are limited, and I can take comfort in knowing the junk will leave when she leaves. I wish I did not have to think like that because we genuinely love when my parents come to visit. The truth is, I cannot control her thoughts and ideas, and when I witness that behavior even 5,000 miles from her own house, it is a discouraging reminder that she is still a hoarder.

I get all warm and fuzzy inside when we not only have friends over, but when our daughter is able to have her friends over. I feel a sense of pride when she takes them up to her room and shows off her toys. I am not great at entertaining but I love to do it – just because I can – and I love when people sleep over. I love that we can run around the house, do forward rolls and handstands, and simply sit and lay on the floor – just because we can. I love to cook meals and bake goodies in my own kitchen – just because I can. I love to do home projects and mundane weekly cleaning chores – just because I can. Some days I will stop everything and just look around our humble little "starter home" and our yard and at our clean, empty cars, and thank God for not only what we have, but for all the *space*.

I remember walking all over the neighborhood, selling Girl Scout cookies with my dad, year after year, smelling the unfamiliar scents of home cooking wafting through the open doors and windows. I would timidly peek into people's houses and stare at the soft, lush grass in their yards, wide-eyed, seeing how nicely they lived. Cars were parked in their ports…the doorbell worked…they could open the door all the way…there were no stacks of newspapers or boxes…there was carpet…someone was comfortably relaxing on a couch watching television…

I still find myself admiring other people's houses more than what would probably considered "normal." Even the most modest abodes excite me when they're clean and tidy. I am more impressed by that than expensive décor, and could seriously not care less where you got your home furnishings, as long as there is room to sit and walk, and I can close the bathroom door. I am more prone to compliment than criticize someone else's home. I have been in other hoarders' homes and still envied the space they had!

I recently took two personality tests – one for work and one for fun. The results for both were spot-on and told me a lot about myself, but I'm curious how much of it was nature versus nurture? For example, I have always welcomed rules, and thrived where expectations are set for me in black and white. Perhaps the most likely reason for this is because I craved structure in a world of utter chaos and disorder. Further, as much as I hated getting in trouble and feeling guilty, getting reprimanded meant I had been noticed.

My parents always seemed to trust me – too much, I felt, at times. I rarely took advantage of that. I had my vices and made my share of mistakes, but was a good kid overall and I was afraid of getting in trouble (my therapist noted that I have a strong *super-ego*). I was often disciplined and occasionally spanked as a little kid when I would badly misbehave, so I guess that drove some kind of fear into me. Perhaps that's also where my aggressive side comes from? I tend to get physical when I lose my temper, to the point where I have even scared myself in the past. That might be because of the spankings, though I think they also did me some good because I surely learned my place. It actually might have "worked" TOO well. When I got in trouble in school, it was almost always because I talked out of turn or talked back to the teacher. With enough spankings, one in-school suspension, and countless trips to the Principal's Office, by the time I left elementary school, I completely shut up. From seventh grade through college, class participation was always the most terrifying part of the grade; I dreaded opening my mouth during class. I started a new school in seventh grade, so you could blame my "newness" or my pubescent insecurity, but I believe the more probable cause for the change was my conditioning.

But who or where would I be without my parents and the way they raised me? My present reality is influenced directly by my past, for better and for worse. With respect to the latter, I persevere to be a student of any "misfortune" along the way, and not a victim.

The career path I chose right out of college was that of a financial advisor. I chose practicality over any "dreams," though honestly, it was the first opportunity that presented itself to me. I only did it for ten months, and although sales was so NOT for me (it actually created a phone phobia for years after my role changed), it ultimately led to where I am professionally today; but the reason I entered this field in the first place was very personal. In my final interview I was asked why I wanted to be a financial advisor. I said I wanted to help people not only succeed financially, but also avoid the financial ruin my parents experienced.

Here is a blog post I wrote that references their plight, along with some other experiences I will never forget.

The Most Important Thing I Learned in College (March 2011)

In 2001, I left home and went off to college. I packed one huge suitcase, one small suitcase, one small box, and a (heavy) backpack, and flew 5,000 miles away from everything I'd ever known, to live in a state I had never previously visited. I had no idea what to expect. I was terrified and excited at the same time.

Thankfully, my mom came with me. She had a friend in NYC who offered to put us up in her spare studio apartment for the two weeks prior to school starting, so we took her up on that. I loved "life" in NYC – from riding the subway, to seeing the Statue of Liberty up close – but knowing I was not going home, I suffered through a pretty severe homesickness. I could not sleep or eat at all (the inability to eat was a real shame because our hostess owned a Chinese restaurant, and she graciously fed us pretty much the entire time we were there!), and I had a weird, nagging ache in my stomach.

By the time I finally "adjusted," it was time to drive down to PA and start my college adventure. I am grateful for that buffer period between leaving home and starting school, because I would have been such an embarrassing, unproductive, miserable mess! I still really missed everyone and everything back home, and that would never change, but I was OK. I was functional again, at least. But the worst was yet to come.

Move-in day will go down in history as one of the worst days of my entire life. My mom and I arrived at my dorm hall, with my suitcases, box, backpack, and the computer I had just purchased, and when I gave them my name to check in… My name was on the "REJECT" list due to financial issues that had to be taken up with the Financial Aid/Student Accounts department.

Dumbfounded, we wandered over to that office, and discovered that I was not allowed to move in because my parents had not sent in any money for housing.

My parents did not have the money. They had BOTH just lost their jobs, and had declared bankruptcy. My dad had read something the Financial Aid office had sent with all the other paperwork about "Special Circumstances," and mistakenly, innocently, thought we would automatically qualify for that, not knowing that it was a whole separate application process. He figured between that and the loans I had qualified for (which covered maybe 1/3 of the cost), everything was taken care of. My mom was completely clueless because my dad handled all the bills. Well, the heartless guy we initially talked to could not have cared less. I will never forget him saying, "Well, if you can write us a check right now for $5,000, you'll be able to move in. Otherwise, sorry." No emotion. No sympathy. He apathetically shrugged his shoulders when I explained that my airplane ticket was one way, said he had to get to the orientation, and left us alone.

Although I am an emotional person, I rarely cry, especially in public. I bawled. Hard. I cried for probably an hour straight, as we made our way to orientation ourselves, and my mom and I called my dad who was back in Hawai`i, explaining what had happened. I remember starting the conversation, and then becoming incoherent through my sobs, and giving the phone to my heartbroken, helpless mother. My dad felt horrible. He blamed himself for the whole thing, and in desperation, prayed that it would work out, even though he was not a man of faith.

What happened next is all a blur. A kind soul saw my mom and me in the lobby of the gym, on the phone forever, me still sobbing. He/she asked my mom if I was OK, and she briefly explained what had happened. That person told us to wait there, and came back a couple minutes later with the head of Student Accounts, who graciously left the orientation and took us back to her office to see how/if she could help. This woman knew nothing about me, but for some reason, she saw "promise" in me, and wanted to give me a chance. She agreed to let me stay if 1) I could come up with part of the initial deposit on the spot (I don't even remember how much it was, but I had enough in my own savings account to pay it at that moment), and 2) I would work on campus starting that week and directly deposit 100% of my earnings towards my tuition/housing bill. It was a deal. I moved in, and had a job – the highest paying job on campus, at that.

I was eventually granted that "Special Circumstance," after going through the application process, which did cut a little bit off my tuition. My first year, I worked 20 hours/week (the max you were allowed as a student worker during the school year), and gave every last penny to Student Accounts. I stayed on campus through the summer, and worked 40 hours because room and board became free when you worked on campus full-time during the summer months. I applied every one of those pennies toward my bill, too. I drained my savings account to buy a very used car for $500 cash (plus some extra for repairs), and got a second part-time job off campus to pay for books and travel. Between both jobs, I started putting in roughly 40 hours a week during the school year. I stayed on campus to work every summer, 50-60 hours a week between both jobs. I studied my butt off to keep up my grades so I wouldn't lose my partial scholarship.

In May of 2005, I graduated Magna cum Laude, and had a zero balance on my bill.

Yes, I am still repaying some federal student loans, and will be for a very long time, but that's OK. It was my choice to attend a private institution, so I accept that responsibility. I don't blame my dad, or anyone, for what happened. The whole experience taught me the value of perseverance and hard work, and should be a testament to all that, where there's a will, there REALLY IS a way. This was probably the greatest lesson I learned in college. I also learned that there ARE nice people in the world…and it can be both humbling and liberating when you accept their help.

A couple days before graduation, I wrote a heartfelt thank-you letter to that head of Student Accounts. I told her she was my angel, that I couldn't have done it without her, and that I would never forget her. She evidently didn't forget me, either, because she contacted me a couple years later about a job opportunity. I was so sad to learn that she recently passed away, but her kind deed will forever live on in my memory.

As for my dad's prayer… I later found out that my dad had made a deal with God – yeah, we all know how much He loves when we do that! – that if I were allowed to stay at that school, he would start going to church with my mom. God quickly answered his prayer, and my dad kept his side of the bargain. Shortly after that, he actually became a Christian himself! He is now very active in the church, and even occasionally leads the adult Sunday school. I like to say that my "worst day" was well worth it in the end, because it led to my dad's salvation…not that I'd ever want to live through it again.

Ten years later, I am still in PA. It was never my intention to stay here after I graduated, but God had different plans for me…at least for now. I was offered a job right out of college, and was in a serious relationship that eventually turned into a marriage that is going on its fifth year. I am still homesick, but I survive. I fly home at least every other year to see the same friends and family that I still miss as much as I did the first day I left.

I count my blessings every day because God has provided for me immeasurably, but I continue to make sacrifices. I know that He gives, and He takes away, but I will always have control over my stewardship. I am so thankful this was ingrained into me at a young age. I hate what happened financially to my parents, but I have learned from their blight, and am encouraged to be a million times more careful than I would be otherwise.

When it became within my control, I swore to myself that I would never put myself or my family through the financial hell my parents experienced and continue to struggle through. I'd had no idea how serious the situation until they filed for bankruptcy. My dad always withheld bad news from me to protect me, so I would not worry. I did worry, but it really became my own personal "burden" when they could not pay for any part of my wedding, and we cover their airfare whenever they come to visit. It was challenging starting my adult life without any sort of fiscal assistance, especially when the majority of my friends were taken care of (some with no student loans, even), but I cannot resent my parents because it was my choice to move away and attend a private university. I am also grateful to them for everything they WERE able to provide for me throughout my life, plus I learned to be thrifty and appreciate the little things.

I try to be very careful with our finances, and refuse to voluntarily go into debt to live beyond our means. We clip coupons when we can and shop around for deals. If a large, unexpected purchase or repair is inevitable, we scale back on whatever we can until we recover. We save. We tithe. We eat out infrequently. I regularly shop at consignment stores and sales. I thank God daily for our jobs that pay our bills, and we both work hard so as to never jeopardize our positions. That's not to say my parents did not do all that, too; but in the end, they were spending more than they were making, and by the time they both lost their jobs, it was too late to catch up. I cannot allow myself to follow that path.

There are other traits or behaviors of my parents – mostly Mom's – that I have to be careful to not adopt. As I get older, I catch myself sounding like her or reacting like her in undesirable ways. For one thing, I hear her "voice" whenever I yell at or scold my daughter or husband. She also sometimes makes jokes that aren't funny or says something that normally would not elicit laughter, and then chuckles nervously. I do that. A LOT. I notice that I get uncomfortable the instant I say something that was unintentionally stupid or not funny but delivered as though it should be. It is very awkward!

Also awkward is when I feel the need to be "strict" with my mother to protect her from herself. There is a thin line between concerned confrontation and disrespectful criticism, especially where your parents are concerned. Mom must realize that it is not the latter, but when tough love is given it is only because all other options and methods have been exhausted. None of us want to see her self-destruct.

This is sometimes necessary in her everyday life. Without my dad, I sometimes wonder if Mom would ever make it anywhere on time. In *Dirty Secret*, Sholl relates. In one exchange with her mother, she asks her, "'How much time can that take?' 'You have no idea.' She shakes her head as if it's the saddest thing in the world [...] Excessive slowness, it turns out, is not uncommon among hoarders. They're often slow in completing tasks and late for appointments. At least in my mother's case, the slowness is partly due to indecisiveness—each and every movement has to be considered and carefully weighed—and partly due to perfectionism and anxiety (worry about somehow making the wrong move)" (p. 58).

Or it is someone else's fault. Mom is always a victim and is quick to blame others. Everyone lets her down. Throughout my own life I have found myself playing the victim in way too many situations. Incase you didn't know, let me be the first to tell you, that game wins no sympathy. In fact, it had the exact opposite effect of what I sought. Though I am not sure she would admit to needing validation like I do, I think this is what my mother needs, too. The trouble is, after a while, people stop feeling sorry for you or trying to defend you because frankly, it just gets annoying. I know from experience! You come across as impossible to please and people start walking on eggshells around you for fear of your villainizing them. People avoid my mom now because she does this very thing. I got tired of that mindset once I realized what I was doing to the people in my life, and how lonely I was becoming.

One positive lesson my mom instilled in me was to leave a place better than you found it. Even as a child I found that ironic, considering the state of their house; nevertheless, she did a great job leading by example – wiping down counters left wet or dirty, flushing someone else's toilet, picking up and throwing away trash, leaving a hotel room with nothing worse than a slightly unmade bed and a full wastebasket, and so on. To this day I follow this ideology, and will teach my children to at least try to do the same. As long as you wash your hands well afterwards, what's the harm, right? I do, however, have to be careful to not become judgmental of others for not holding themselves to a similar standard. This proves to be especially difficult for me when we have (adult) visitors in our home who leave behind messes... I am not sure I will ever be fully OK with this, but I digress. It does not mean I cannot do my part!

Another thing I admire about my mother is her thoughtfulness. She is one of the most thoughtful people I know, remembering everyone's birthdays and keeping others on her mind at all times. She is always finding or making little gifts or trinkets for friends and family. But she has an odd way of giving those gifts. In many instances she has unceremoniously tossed items in my direction without explanation, then when I look at it curiously or ask what it is, she says, "You have one of those? I thought you could use that for such-and-such" and goes on to enthusiastically explain where she found it or why she thought of me when she saw it. She is so proud of her finds and the fact that she can express she was thinking of you, it is hard to feel or respond negatively when she gives you something out of the blue like that – but the tossing of the thing kind of kills the mood.

I am personally terrible at gift-giving, and have been known to leave gifts for people with a note/card when they're not around – sometimes on purpose, for fear of seeing them hate it when they see it. The problem with that for an individual in search of validation is that you're silently tortured by the question of whether or not they a) got the gift and b) liked it. I have caught myself explaining why and where I got the gift – like my mom does – when it is positively accepted. When it's not, I apologize and offer to exchange or return it. One key difference between us is that I am OK with people returning what I buy them if they really don't want it. (Gift receipts really are a wonderful thing!) My mom, on the other hand, comes across as offended and defeated if I so much as question an odd purchase or discourage her from spending her money on something I will never use, so now I usually just keep my mouth shut.

One last challenge involves my efforts to stay in touch with friends and family. I'm so thankful for social media and email because frankly, I hate calling people. I just do. The only people I regularly call to spontaneously chat are my parents. But for the longest time, they did not call me. It has always been tough to synchronize our schedules because of the time difference between Hawai`i and Pennsylvania (they are 5-6 hours behind, depending on Daylight Savings), but at least I keep trying. Until recently, they would only call on my birthday or special holidays like

Christmas, but otherwise did not bother, and that was nothing short of disappointing. I asked them repeatedly to call me once in a while, reminding them that I am their only child, but still they would not call. They do call more often now, though when we do talk, Mom tends to ramble unless I take charge of the conversation. It seems difficult for her to stay focused on a topic without getting wrapped up in minute details. She also often seems disinterested when I talk.

I do not want to be like that. Without smothering my children, I have every intention of seeing or calling (or texting…or whatever we're doing in 15 years from now) them on a regular basis, even if it is just to let them know I am always thinking of them and love them so very dearly. I never want that to be a doubt in their minds for a second, no matter how old they are.

My life thus far has been a pretty loud indication of how important a mother's evident love and care are to a child. I have my work cut out for me, but thanks again to therapy, a patient husband, and the other supportive people in my life, I know I am better today than I was and have chosen to continue healing. What is a "normal" life? I think I am finally finding out, and am excited and optimistic about the years ahead of me.

Conclusion

Each and every one of us has a unique and impactful story to tell. Each and every one of us – no matter what kind of home life, parents, education, or economic class one has hailed from – can enrich the lives of others in a myriad of ways, big and small. We can learn from each other by sharing our struggles and our victories, our pain and our joy, our failures and our discoveries. And no matter how rough your story starts, each and every one of us has the power to re-write the ending. We cannot change our past and we may not be able to change our present circumstances, but we CAN change our attitude and our outlook on life. It is not easy, but it is worth it. YOU are worth it.

There will come the inevitable day, hopefully far off, where it will be my sole responsibility to clean out my parents' home when they are gone. I am not looking forward to the time and labor that will be required, but at the same time, that will be my final liberation from this nightmare. Until then, I hope and pray that my mom realizes healing and freedom from her own bondage to her possessions. May she find peace regardless of whether or not she ever finds the validation she seeks. May she be happy and healthy and safe…because SHE is worth it.

I know God is not finished with me yet, and I have got a very long way to go in this journey, but I vow to continue to learn and grow for the sake of my family's well-being, and my own…because THEY are worth it.

And so am I.

VALIDATE ME!

Bibliography

Sources are listed in order of appearance. All website material was personally reviewed and cited in August 2013.

Children of Hoarders.
http://childrenofhoarders.com

Hoarders.org: "Definition of Hoarding."
http://www.hoarders.org.

Mayo Clinic: "Hoarding – Definition."
http://www.mayoclinic.com/health/hoarding/DS00966.

Frisch, Steve, PsyD. Addiction in Family: "Core Issues For Children of Alcoholics." http://addictioninfamily.com/family-issues/core-issues-for-children-of-alcoholics/.

Whitfield, Charles L., M.D. *Healing The Child Within: Discovery and Recovery for Adult Children of Dysfunctional Families.* Deerfield Beach, FL: Health Communications, Inc. 1987.

International OCD Foundation: "From Dante to DSM-V: A Short History of Hoarding."
http://www.ocfoundation.org/hoarding/hoarding.aspx?id=686&terms=genetics.

Saxena, S. "Is Compulsive Hoarding a Genetically and Neurobiologically Discrete Syndrome? Implications for Diagnostic Classification." *The American Journal of Psychiatry*: Vol. 164, March 2007, pp. 380-84, 493-9.

Saxena, S., Brody AL, Maidment KM, Smith EC, Zohrabi N, Katz E, Baker SK, Baxter LR Jr. "Cerebral Glucose Metabolism in Obsessive-Compulsive Hoarding." *The American Journal of Psychiatry*: Vol. 161, June 2004, pp. 1038-48.

Frost, Randy, PhD. *Spring 2007 New England Hoarding Consortium Newsletter.*
http://www.childrenofhoarders.com/files/NEHC_Newsletter_April_2007.pdf.

Norton, Amy. *Reuters Life*: "Cluttered Home? Blame Your Genes" (2009).
http://mobile.reuters.com/article/lifestyleMolt/idUSTRE59S52720091029.

Tolin, David, Randy O. Frost, and Gail Steketee. *Buried in Treasures: Help for Compulsive Acquiring, Saving, and Hoarding (Treatments That Work)*. New York: Oxford University Press. 2007.

Sholl, Jessie. *Dirty Secret: A Daughter Comes Clean About Her Mother's Compulsive Hoarding.* New York: Gallery Books. 2011.

Acknowledgments

Heartfelt gratitude is expressed to the following for their substantial contributions and support during this entire journey and in the creation of this memoir.

My husband, Billy
Victoria L. Ostroff, Psy.D.
George Searfoss
Nancy Searfoss
Debra Heschl
David Mayer
Suzanne A. Chabaud, Ph.D.
Matt Paxton
Screaming Flea Productions
A&E and the entire "Hoarders" crew
Johnny Harris

Mahalo nui loa.